RAILS ACROSS PANAMA

ALSO BY JOSEPH L. SCHOTT

Above and Beyond: The Story of the Congressional Medal of Honor

Ordeal of Samar

RAILS ACROSS PANAMA

The Story of the Building of the Panama Railroad 1849-1855

JOSEPH L. SCHOTT

THE BOBBS-MERRILL COMPANY, INC.
A SUBSIDIARY OF HOWARD W. SAMS & CO., INC.
PUBLISHERS *Indianapolis • New York • Kansas City*

FIRST PRINTING, 1967

LIBRARY OF CONGRESS CATALOG CARD NUMBER 66-30499

DESIGNED BY JIM PAPPAS
MANUFACTURED IN THE UNITED STATES OF AMERICA

For Mona and Richard Carlson

Prologue

PRIOR TO THE CONSTRUCTION OF THE PANAMA CANAL NO GEOGRAPHical problem frustrated seagoing travelers quite so much as the lack of a convenient passage between the Atlantic and Pacific oceans. From the time that Columbus arrived off Panama in 1502 until the canal was finally completed in the early twentieth century, Central America was the scene of many searches to find the best route across the land barrier. In 1849 a group of American businessmen, considered foolhardy by most of their contemporaries, decided on Panama and began construction of a railroad there.

This book covers in particular the period 1849 to 1855, the height of the California Gold Rush. It deals with the construction of the Panama Railroad and tells the stories of many of the people who came to the Isthmus at that time. The people are all long dead and gone—many buried in the soggy soil of Panama, killed by cholera, the guns of the Derienni, or the rope of a man named Runnels. The original railroad line is also buried, most of it under the waters of Gatun Lake. Now only the memory remains—of the people, the railroad, and the era of the Yankee Strip.

Contents

Illustrations

Illustrations will be found following

pages 114 and 146.

All photographs
courtesy the Library of Congress

"I take up my pen to write this down in an earnest effort to leave behind a small chip or leaf on the Shores of Time, 'ere the small river of my life wends its way to the sea, and is forever lost in the Bounding Main."

OCTAVIA CHARITY MARSDEN, *nee* RUNNELS

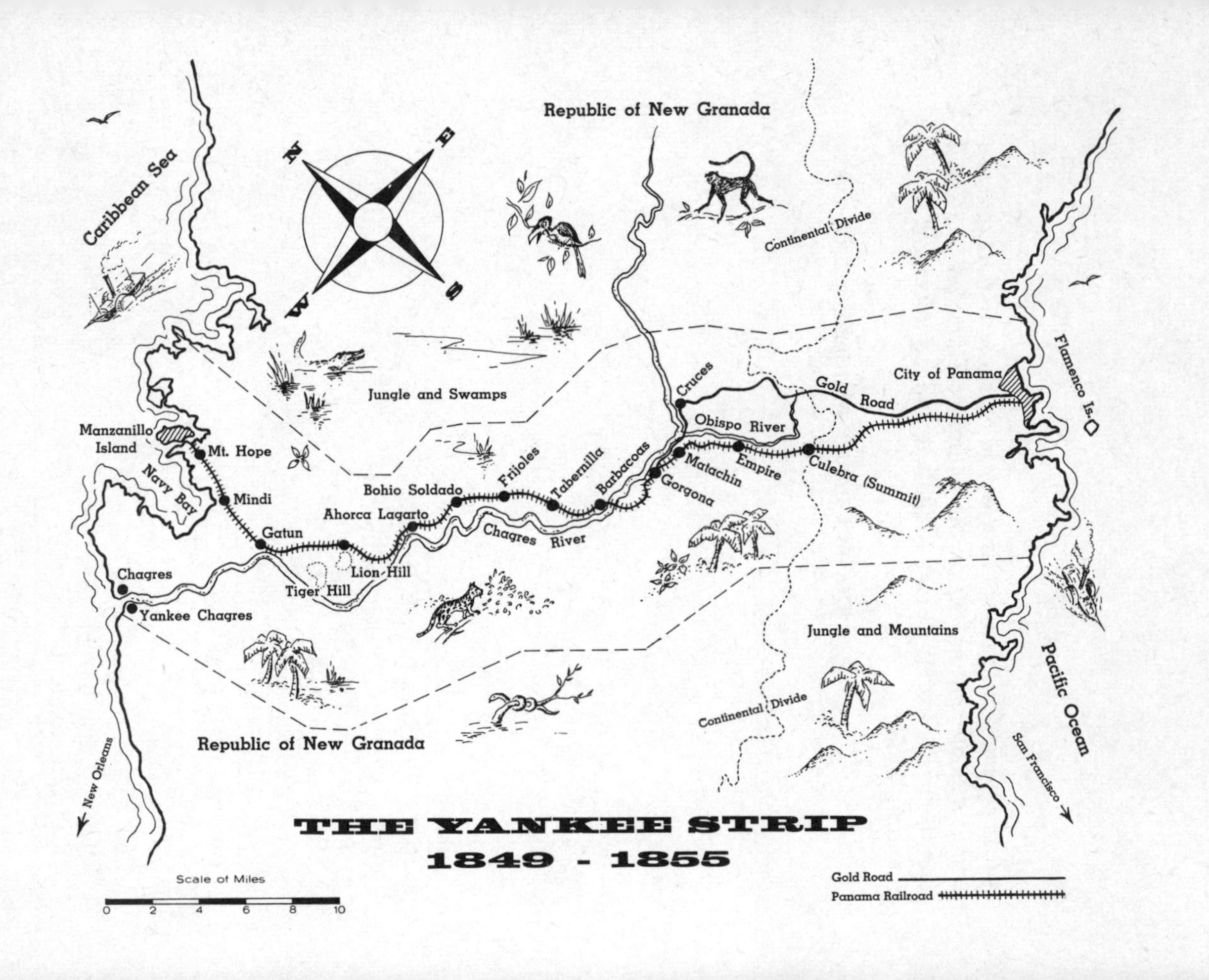

Republic of New Granada
Caribbean Sea
N
E
S
W
Continental Divide
Jungle and Swamps
Manzanillo
Island
Mt. Hope
Navy Bay
Mindi
Gatun
Chagres
Yankee Chagres
Tiger Hill
Lion Hill
Ahorca Lagarto
Bohio Soldado
Frijoles
Tabernilla
Barbacoas
Gorgona
Matachin
Empire
Culebra (Summit)
Cruces
Obispo River
Chagres River
Gold
Road
City of Panama
Flamenco Is.
Jungle and Mountains
Continental Divide
Pacific Ocean
San Francisco
Republic of New Granada
New Orleans
THE YANKEE STRIP
1849 - 1855
Scale of Miles
0 2 4 6 8 10
Gold Road
Panama Railroad

I

The Barrier

As THE SMALL SIDE-WHEEL STEAMER *Falcon* NEARED THE COAST of Central America that day in late December of 1847, most of the passengers at the rail had their first view of the source of bafflement to many a king—a long, low hill across the horizon, a forbidding barrier of land shrouded in gray mist. The *Falcon* was bound for Chagres, the principal port on the Caribbean coast of the Isthmus of Panama. As she moved closer to her destination, intermittent rain squalls swept across her decks. The greenish gray of the sea, undulating in huge swells, turned yellow and then dark brown with the discharge from the mouth of a great river. Between showers the veil of mist obscuring the land cleared slightly and the dripping passengers could see high mountains—the Andes of Darien—far to the south. When the *Falcon* splashed her anchor a mile offshore, low-flying gulls, some white and some brown, swept across the deck making mewing sounds, almost like startled kittens.

The river mouth, a quarter of a mile wide, was closed with a line of white foam, betraying the hidden presence of a submerged sand bar. The water covering the bar was less than 13 feet deep at high tide; the *Falcon,* despite her shallow draft, could not cross into the bay formed by the mouth of the river. While waiting for the crew to break out a lighter, the passengers surveyed the shore. They saw the village of Chagres—a group of about 50 cane huts—on the right river bank at the base of a jungle-covered hill and, on the opposite bank, a grove of graceful coconut palms. High on the hill above the village was a pile of crumbling stone overgrown with vines and creepers—the ruins of the ancient fort of San Lorenzo.

At the rail of the *Falcon,* John L. Stephens, a lawyer and writer who had traveled widely in Central America, related to his employer William H. Aspinwall some of the fort's colorful history: how it had been constructed by the Spanish to protect treasure ships in the port of Chagres and had been the last continental stronghold evacuated by Spain after Bolívar's victory at Ayacucho in 1826. The fort's present condition of ruinous neglect, said Stephens, was typical of contemporary affairs on the Isthmus.

Aspinwall, a New York businessman, expressed only mild interest in the recital. He had come to Panama to study the possibilities of constructing a railroad across from sea to sea, not to poke about crumbling ruins.

As they waded ashore from the *Falcon's* lighter through the shallow water to the beach, they had their first full view of the most important port on the Atlantic side of the Isthmus.

"Chagres at this time," wrote the historian Bancroft, "was a town of about seven hundred inhabitants, dwelling in some fifty windowless, bamboo huts, with thatched, palm-leaf roofs, and having open entrances, and the bare ground floor. The town was surrounded by heaps of filthy offal, and greasy, stagnant pools bordered with blue mud."

There were a few adobe houses scattered among the cane huts. Stephens explained that these were relics of the Spanish era, and said also that the soggy streets of Chagres had once been paved with stones, but the paving was long buried under the deep layer of mud. "Nothing of a progressive nature has occurred here since the departure of the Spanish in 1826," he said. "We must realize at all times that we are dealing with a population as backward as any on the face of the earth."

The population, mainly Indians and Negroes clad in scanty cotton garments, stood in the muddy streets smoking cigars and watching the new arrivals with sleepy interest. Naked children, also smoking cigars, scampered about, scattering pigs and dogs. Led by Stephens, the group walked from the landing place on the beach, slapping at mosquitoes and huge flying cockroaches, to the only hostelry in Chagres. According to the traveler Osborne, this was "a house, called a hotel, kept by Peter Eskildsen, who professed to use his utmost endeavours to facilitate to travelers all of the conveniences that the country will permit of." Eskildsen, a Scandinavian sailor stranded in Panama by his captain as punishment for a breach of shipboard discipline, had taken up with a native woman in Chagres and settled down. Since the country had few conveniences to offer, Eskildsen was not strained in furnishing them to travelers. His hotel was a cane hut, indistinguishable from the other huts except that it was slightly larger and occupied a central position in the village. The floors were dirt, the windows were unscreened, the travelers slept on hammocks slung from the roof poles, and the hotel had just as great a population of fleas and rats as the other huts.

Aspinwall was fortunate in having along a traveler with the experience of John L. Stephens. At Stephens' insistence the group had brought a large supply of preserved foods: pickles, dried fruit, ham and jelly, as well as bottles of wine and mineral water. With these delicacies they were able to vary the standard local diet of pork, bread and bananas.

The classic route across the Isthmus utilized the rivers and their valleys. From the Caribbean shore one paddled upstream on the Chagres River as far as possible. About two-thirds of the way across, the Chagres forked with its principal tributary, the Obispo. The Chagres valley swung back northeast while the

Obispo valley continued southeast toward the Continental Divide. Just across the divide from the headwaters of the Obispo began the tortuous valley of the Rio Grande, which snaked down the southern slope to the Pacific at Panama City. The configuration of these almost-connecting river valleys had made them a trade route across the Isthmus since the earliest times.

Traveling up the Chagres in bungos poled by native boatmen, the Aspinwall party found they could reach the village of Gorgona —39½ river miles from Chagres—in three days. By traveling another full day on the river they could reach the village of Cruces. Cruces was only four and a half miles beyond Gorgona, but the current suddenly became much swifter and slowed the boats considerably. From Cruces they followed the muddy, neglected trace of an old Spanish gold trail, up the Obispo valley, over the divide, and then down the steep Rio Grande valley to Panama City.

After several conferences with Stephens and the party engineer, James L. Baldwin, Aspinwall decided that digging a ship canal across Panama was not feasible—it would cost too much money. But Aspinwall became convinced that a railroad *could* be constructed there. Prior to leaving New York, he had been told by railroad builders that if the maximum elevation of the divide he had to cross was higher than 600 feet above sea level, the operation of a railroad would be impossible; the slope of the roadbed would be too steep to hold the wheels to the rails. Baldwin had found a pass in the divide just 300 feet above sea level, well below the maximum. Baldwin had also expressed the professional opinion that specially built shallow-draft steamers, carrying passengers and freight, could penetrate upstream on the Chagres as far as Gorgona even during the dry season. Encouraged by these facts and opinions, Aspinwall decided to build a single-track railroad line from Gorgona on the Chagres to Panama City on the Pacific. Passengers and baggage could then be sent from ocean to ocean by a combination of steamer and rail service. After this interim system was operating and earning revenue, the railroad line from the Atlantic side to

Gorgona—a section where the swampy terrain presented many complicated roadbed problems—could be surveyed and constructed in a deliberate manner.

Before leaving the Isthmus, it was the pleasure of the erudite Stephens to take the men of business, Aspinwall and his associate Henry Chauncey, on a tour of the fortress of San Lorenzo. With several naked native children as guides they marched across the bottom of the ravine below the fortress and up the narrow path leading to the base of the walls. Inside the moss-covered outer ring of stone which had served as the first line of defense, they faced other massive walls, pocked with tiny air vents almost hidden in the foliage. The drawbridge, which had once clanged down so authoritatively, now lay at a drunken angle in the debris-filled moat, so they had to cross on a swaying rope bridge to reach the base of the tower. As they pushed through the thickets growing from cracks in the stone paving, they stumbled over the rusty barrels of dismounted cannon and conical piles of cannon balls. Inside the tower they found, according to Stephens, muddy dungeon cells with iron fetters "weighing forty pounds or more to clamp about a prisoner's ankle, or, for that matter, his neck."

"Mr. Aspinwall," said Stephens, "unmoved by the past cruelties of the Dons, as displayed by these rings of iron, was most interested in the effects of the climate on the metal since he would be responsible for the purchase of the rails to be used on the road. Mr. Chauncey stopped frequently to make notes on how the railroad company should be financed, trying to effect a balance between the shares of stock to be issued and the bonded indebtedness to be attached to the operating equipment." The saga of the Panama railway had begun.

II

The Dream of Kings

THE UNITED STATES HAD BEEN INTERESTED IN ACQUIRING THE RIGHTS of passage across a section of Central America for the construction of a railroad or a canal for many years. In 1835 President Andrew Jackson appointed Charles Biddle of Philadelphia as a special emissary to explore Panama and Nicaragua for possible routes. Biddle went to Panama in November 1835 and crossed the Isthmus in four days by way of the Chagres and the old Spanish trail. He died in Philadelphia shortly afterward from fever contracted on the trip, his surveys uncompleted.

In 1839 President Martin Van Buren sent John L. Stephens to Central America to continue the Biddle surveys. Stephens, personable and intelligent, and fluent in the Spanish language, was accompanied by his friend the British artist Frederick Catherwood. During this journey, and a second one in 1841, Stephens and Catherwood traveled through many of the Central American states, often at great personal risk because of the numerous bloody revolutions. Stephens wrote down detailed descriptions of the topography and the customs of the inhabitants, and Catherwood drew sketches. In addition to canal and railroad routes, they explored archeological wonders, including the ruins of the ancient, half-buried city of Copán in Honduras. The only immediate result of their journeys was the publication of Stephens' book, *Incidents of Travel in Central America, Chiapas and Yucatan* with its famous Catherwood drawings, which remains a standard work in Mayan archeology.

The trip of the New York businessman William H. Aspinwall to Panama in 1847 was the direct result of a move by the United States Government earlier that year to subsidize steamship mail service from New York and New Orleans to the isolated settlements on the Pacific Coast. It is difficult today to comprehend how far that coast was from the Eastern Seaboard in the middle of the nineteenth century. The trip overland across the continent took three months, as did the sailing ship voyage around Cape Horn. In an attempt to speed up transcontinental mail service, the Government decided to connect mail steamers in the opposite oceans by a permanent, serviceable passageway across Central America, the narrow but maddening barrier that had frustrated the political and economic ambitions of the enlightened rulers of the world for years.

Late in 1846 the United States negotiated a treaty with the Colombian Confederation—a union of several Latin American states which included the Republic of New Granada, the country which had sovereignty over the Isthmus of Panama—and received the right of free and uninterrupted transit from "the one to the other sea" anywhere across the Isthmus in the area between the Chiriqui Lagoon and the Atrato River, a distance of over 400 miles. In return for this concession, the United States recognized the sovereignty of the Colombian Confederation and New Granada over the Isthmus. Control of the area by the central government at Bogotá had been rather shaky in the past. As recently as 1831 a local revolutionary government had taken over Panama, and with tacit British approval tried to free it from the federation. Peace had been restored only after much bloody fighting. This experience caused Bogotá to welcome a treaty with the United States that would recognize confederation supremacy on the Isthmus.

On April 20, 1847, Secretary of the Navy John Mason awarded a contract to one Albert G. Sloo of Cincinnati for the operation of "a line of steamships, to consist of at least five vessels, for the transportation of the United States Mail from New York City to New Orleans . . . touching at Charleston, Savannah and Havana, and from Havana to Chagres and back, twice a month. . . ." The concession to Sloo was to run ten years and granted him an annual mail subsidy of $290,000. The following August, Sloo, who was apparently a speculator without sufficient funds or credit to handle the project himself, sold the contract to a group of New York capitalists headed by George Law—a canal, bridge and railroad builder who had amassed a fortune and founded New York City's horsecar transit company.

The Navy contract as purchased by Law contained specifications and restrictions regarding the construction and the operation of the vessels to be used. "The said steamship is to be of not less than fifteen hundred tons burden, and propelled by engines of not less than one thousand horse power each, and is to be constructed under the superintendence and direction of a Naval Constructor in the employ of the Navy Department, and constructed as to render the conversion at the least possible expense into a war steamer of the first class. . . . The said boilers and machinery are to be of the first quality and so placed below the water line as to be as far as practicable beyond the reach of cannon shot. . . . Each and all of said steamships shall be commanded by an officer of the Navy of the United States not below the grade of lieutenant and accommodated or housed thereof in a manner becoming his rank and station, without charge to the government of the United States." The Government had decided to reap as a fringe benefit to the mail contract the opportunity to train some Navy officers in steam navigation.

On May 4, 1847, Secretary Mason advertised for bids on a

monthly mail contract, also valid for ten years, for service along the Pacific Coast between Panama City and Astoria, Oregon. This contract did not excite much interest. The distance to be covered was twice as great as the New York to Chagres run and the West Coast was sparsely settled. Also, the Mexican War was still in progress and California had not yet become irrevocably a territory of the United States. The trading posts and ranches on the Pacific Coast produced a scanty flow of furs, hides and lumber for export, and bulky shipments would have to go around Cape Horn anyway because transportation across the rugged Isthmus terrain was possible only by mules and small river boats. Another speculator, Arnold Harris from Arkansas, won the contract with a bid for $199,000 annual subsidy and immediately sold it to William H. Aspinwall, who founded the Pacific Mail Steamship Company. This contract called for the same general Navy specifications as the Atlantic contract, but permitted smaller ships, "not less than one thousand tons burden," to be constructed.

Many of his conservative business associates did not undertand why Aspinwall, a partner in the highly successful clipper ship firm of Howland and Aspinwall, would invest a large sum in a scheme which seemed to offer no hope of immediate profit. The Government mail subsidy was not large enough to pay the full cost of founding a steamship line and the population on the Pacific Coast was growing too slowly to generate a profitable passenger or express business in the near future. "The Pacific Mail Company," reported a writer of the era, "was looked upon by the generality of businessmen as a sequestration of a large amount of property for an indefinite time, with a faint prospect of profit; and the wonder seemed to be that so sound a man as Mr. Aspinwall should have engaged in it."

But the sound Mr. Aspinwall had more in mind than merely to found a steamship company serving the Pacific Coast. His basic aim was to construct and control a canal or railroad across the Isthmus of Panama. If he could create and control such an interoceanic passage, shortening the vast distance from the western world to the Pacific Ocean and the Orient, he would accomplish what kings had not, and become one of the most powerful shipping tycoons in the world. His main problem was the Isthmus itself, the terrible Isthmus of Panama.

The exact geographical position of the Isthmus is not understood by most people even today. Knowing that it is part of the dangling land connective between North and South America, they erroneously assume that it runs north and south. This is not so. At Panama the land barrier, narrowing to a width of less than 50 miles, makes a double curve like a hook or a flattened "S". This curving causes the Isthmus to run east and west rather than north and south. North of the Isthmus are the Caribbean Sea and the Atlantic; south lies the Pacific Ocean.

Climatic and geographical problems make the Isthmus formidable despite its narrowness. On the Atlantic side the land is low and flat, covered with swampy jungle and rain forest. Inland from the Atlantic the ground rises gradually to the bony ridge of the Continental Divide—12,000 feet high in some places. From the divide the land falls away precipitately southward to the Pacific, ten miles away.

No place on the globe has a higher average annual rainfall. Lying nine degrees north of the equator, the Isthmus receives most of this rain from June through December. During these months the sun is almost directly overhead, causing a current of warm, moist air to ascend as vapor. Condensing in the cool upper atmosphere, the vapor returns to earth in torrents of rain. The rainfall and the rugged terrain have traditionally discouraged wayfarers crossing there. Numerous rivers, originating on the high ridges of the interior mountains, rush to the sea. Cloudbursts sometimes last three days and create floods which surge downstream through the narrow river valleys like miniature tidal waves. The principal river running to the Caribbean is the Chagres. Prior to its being dammed to form Gatun Lake—the supply lake which feeds the northern locks of the Panama Canal—the Chagres was the uncontrollable villain of the Isthmus. In its narrower canyons the river level could rise 50 feet in two or three hours and drop as rapidly. During the wet months in the pre-canal era the average level of the Chagres was ten feet higher than during the dry months and the volume was unstable, dwindling to a lethargic trickle at times and then rising without warning to flood and sweep away everything in its path.

During the months of solar movement, January and May, rains are moderate on the Isthmus. Then, from February through April, while the sun is far to the south, there is little or no precipitation, and the climate can be very pleasant. The mild character of this dry hiatus has seduced many a traveler who has seen the area only during this season.

Following instructions of William H. Aspinwall, John L. Stephens hurried to Bogotá in early 1848 to obtain a concession for his company in Panama. As Stephens knew well, the idea of building a railroad there had been discussed for some time. In 1841 a French surveyor named Sablá had made a survey for a rail route and in 1845 a French company, organized to build the road, obtained a 99-year concession from New Granada. But economic panic in Europe in 1848 had killed the project, so the Bogotá officials were ready to negotiate with another builder. The contract obtained by Stephens in 1848, which was reaffirmed in a slightly modified form in 1850, embodied the following main points:

1. The Panama Railroad Company would have the exclusive right to build a railroad, highway or canal across the Isthmus, and the exclusive right to operate steam-powered vessels on the Chagres River. No other group would be allowed to engage in any of these activities without the consent of the company.

2. The contract was to continue in force for 49 years—subject to the right of New Granada to take possession of the road at the end of 20 years after completion on payment of $5,000,000, at the end of 30 years for $4,000,000, and at the end of 40 years for $2,000,000.

3. All public lands on the line of the road were to be used gratuitously by the railroad.

4. The construction work was to be completed within eight years.

5. The railroad was to receive a gift of 250,000 acres of public land, to be selected by the railroad from any public lands on the Isthmus.

6. Two ports, one on the Atlantic end and the other on the Pacific, were to be free ports.

7. The railroad had the exclusive right to fix tolls.

8. Three per cent of all declared dividends were to be paid to the Government of New Granada.

9. The railroad company was to put $120,000 in escrow as "earnest" money at the commencement of the contract, but this amount was to be refunded with interest on completion of the road within the given period.

While these mundane business transactions were being conducted, gold was discovered in the mill race at Sutter's Mill, California, on January 24, 1848. The word was slow in getting to the East Coast, however. In April William H. Aspinwall, still unaware of the gold discovery, formally chartered his Pacific Mail Steamship Company with initial capital of $500,000, while his conservative associates predicted failure. He had three ships under construction with which to begin the Pacific Coast service: the *California,* the *Oregon* and the *Panama.* They were wooden paddle-wheel steamers, of approximately the same size—about 200 feet in length and 34 feet in the beam, excluding the paddle-wheels. Each had three masts so that sails could be used in event of engine failure. The individual capacities of these vessels were each about 1,000 tons. With only three steamers it would be impossible to maintain monthly mail service from Panama City to a port as far distant as Astoria, Oregon, so the Secretary of the Navy permitted the company to make San Francisco the northern steamship terminus temporarily. Mail would be sent from there to Oregon by sailing ship, an arrangement that remained in force for about a year until more steamers were built.

The first of the Pacific Mail steamers—the *California*—was launched May 19, 1848. Built by the William H. Webb Company of New York at a cost of $200,082, she had two decks, a round stern, an overhanging bow terminating in a bowsprit, and a capacity of 1,057 tons. The Webb Company was a builder of famous clipper ships, so like all Webb-built vessels the *California* had a beautifully shaped hull. She departed from the port of New York bound for California around Cape Horn on October 6, 1848. Although gold had now been discovered almost eight months and stories had reached the Eastern Seaboard in July, the public was not yet excited, because the first reports gave no indication of the vast extent of the deposits. No one paid much attention when the new steamship left on her maiden voyage. Although the *California* had cabin accommodations for 50 to 60 first-class passengers and bunk space in the steerage for from 150 to 200 more, she sailed with only a few of her spaces filled. These passengers were bound for Rio de Janeiro and Valparaiso; there were none at all for the Pacific Coast. Most of her hold space was taken up with a complete spare set of engine machinery and a year's supply of provisions, there being no repair facilities or victualing stations on the Pacific Coast. Her heavily loaded fuel bunkers, filled with 520 tons of coal, made her ride low in the water and slowed the paddles. Despite the load, she could make ten knots an hour under steam and reached Rio in 26 days—a new steamship record. There she lay over for three weeks to take on more coal and make engine repairs.

While the *California* rode at anchor in the harbor at Rio, waves of hysteria began emanating from Washington. During the weeks that the California steamed south, more and more stories of the gold discovery had appeared in Eastern newspapers. They had been read and commented upon, but roused no widespread excitement. Then, on December 5, 1848, in his message to Congress, President James K. Polk mentioned the official Army report on California gold. Polk said: "It was known that mines of the precious metals existed in California at the time of its acquisition. Recent discoveries render it probable that these mines are more extensive and valuable than was anticipated. The accounts of the abundance of gold in that territory are of such extraordinary character as would scarcely countenance belief were they not corroborated by the authentic reports of officers in the public service, who have visited the mineral districts. . . . The explorations already warrant the belief that the supply of gold is very large. . . ." The Army messenger delivering the report had brought with him also a small chest containing "about $3,000 worth of gold in lumps and scales." This visible treasure was put on display at the War Office in Washington. Growing crowds gathered daily to stare, and to become infected with the new disease—gold fever.

The New York *Journal of Commerce* described current conditions in California: "People are picking gold out of the earth just like a thousand hogs let loose in a forest would root up ground nuts!"

"Root, hog, or die!" yelled the first victims of gold fever and began buying shovels and treasure chests. The rush began to pick up momentum.

Before President Polk's speech, the main problem of George Law, President of the U. S. Mail Steam Line, had been the shipyards' delay in delivery of his new steamers. In desperation, to comply with the time clause of his mail contract, Law chartered the small steamer *Falcon* for the first run to Chagres, to connect with the expected arrival of the *California* at Panama City. The *Falcon* sailed from New York a few days after President Polk's speech with 29 passengers bearing tickets to California—mostly government employees and missionaries. She docked at New Orleans on December 18, to find the dock crowded with 178 hysterical gold-seekers clamoring for passage to Panama. They all carried picks and shovels and, naturally, large bags and buckets in which to bring home their treasure.

Captain Notestein of the *Falcon* also found General Persifor E. Smith, the newly appointed commander of the U. S. Army in California, impatiently waiting to board with his staff. After providing General Smith with first-class quarters, Captain Notestein tried to limit the number of additional passengers to 100—the number of bunks available—and almost started a war. The crowd threatened to storm the ship. Notestein finally rigged bunks in the dining room and hold and took the entire group, sailing from New Orleans on December 19. Prior to departure, the U. S.

Mail Line agent handed Captain Notestein a letter from William H. Aspinwall to Captain Cleveland Forbes of the *California,* for delivery at Panama City. Aspinwall gave Forbes instructions to "crowd a little," if there was an overload of California-bound passengers waiting on the Isthmus. Apparently Aspinwall had begun to foresee the size of the westward movement. As the *Falcon* steamed down the Mississippi for the Gulf of Mexico, she was followed by three other crowded steamers—*Crescent City, Orus* and *Isthmus*—and three overloaded sailing ships.

Meanwhile, the *California* was courting disaster trying to get around Cape Horn. She entered the Straits of Magellan on December 7—two days after President Polk's speech—and as usual there was a storm blowing. After a six-day battle with wind and waves and a bare escape from being dashed to bits against the rocky shore at Punta Arenas, the *California* made the turn into the Pacific and steamed northward up the western coast of South America. She arrived in Callao on December 27. Stories of the fabulous gold finds in California had drifted down into South America. A hundred Peruvian passengers booked passage for San Francisco.

When the *California* arrived at Panama City on January 17, 1849, more than three months after leaving New York, she had space for 150 more passengers. More than 1,000 gold-mad Yankees were in town fighting for passage to San Francisco. The offices of the Pacific Mail Steamship Company were thronged with yelling, pushing mobs clamoring for tickets, trying to bribe the clerks with fistfuls of greenbacks, and sometimes threatening them with physical violence.

When the word got around that there were 100 Peruvians on the *California,* a riot broke out in the Pacific Mail offices. Ticket-seekers smashed furniture and fired guns into the ceiling. General Persifor Smith sided with the rioters in demanding that the "foreigners" be put off the ship to make room for "true blue Americans."

William A. Nelson, a partner in the firm of Zachrisson and Nelson, agents for the Pacific Mail Line, was U. S. Consul in

Panama City. He flatly refused the general's demands, citing the law of precedence on common carriers—first come, first served.

Aboard the *California* the Peruvians, aware that they were the center of controversy, refused to go ashore during the steamer's stay in Panama. While the ship lay at anchor off the harbor island of Taboga, trying to re-coal and re-victual from lighters, she was constantly surrounded by boatloads of frantic supplicants waving money at the uniformed officers on the bridge. Occasionally, a group brave with alcohol would storm the rails of the ship. The mates and boatswains would grab clubs and belaying pins to fight them off. During these forays the water around the ship seethed with fully clothed men, gasping and splashing about, trying to claw up the side of the steamer or get back into their boats.

At the Pacific Mail office William Nelson put the names of ticket-seekers into a hat and held a lottery for the vacant berths. As each name was drawn, the lucky winner—who paid $200 for his fare to San Francisco—was met with extravagant bids for his ticket. "The Wall Street plan," the press dubbed this procedure. A few of the winners, unable to resist a quick profit, sold their tickets for as much as $1,000, and elected to wait in Panama for another steamer.

Major General Smith, still rankled by the presence of the Peruvians on the *California,* was not mollified. U. S. citizens were being left behind while "foreigners" pushed on ahead to the gold fields. General Smith told Consul Nelson that if he did not remove the Peruvians from the *California* to make room for more U. S. citizens, the general would complain to Washington about the matter; and furthermore, on arrival in California, he would order the Army to exclude the Peruvians "and all other foreigners" from the gold diggings.

Nelson could not legally remove the foreigners under his authority as U. S. Consul or as agent of the Pacific Mail Steamship Company, but he had seen Mr. Aspinwall's instructions "to crowd a little," so he made a concession which went a long way toward salving hurt feelings. Nelson agreed to send an additional Yankee passenger for each foreigner on board. The consul went out to the *California* and in fluent Spanish explained his plan to the nervous Peruvians. They gladly agreed to double up. Makeshift bunks were hastily constructed. When the *California* finally sailed from Panama City on January 31, she had 365 passengers—146 per cent of her registered capacity—many crammed into temporary bunks on the deck and in the holds. And these were in addition to a crew of 36.

The voyage to San Francisco proved even more nerve-racking than the trip around the Horn. Stowaways were found in the coal bunkers; the engine-room crew had sold the space to make a private profit. When the stowaways were ejected and placed in irons, the black gang mutinied. Captain Forbes put in at Mazatlan briefly and left all stowaways and the mutiny ringleaders on the beach. Then the coal supply ran out. Spars, doors, bunks and portions of the deck were ripped up to feed the fire box. By the time the *California* struggled into the harbor at San Francisco on February 28, she was stripped of almost everything combustible. As a final blow, the entire crew, except for one engine-room boy, joined the passengers in the rush down the gangplank for the golden shore. The *California,* stripped and deserted by everyone except Captain Cleveland Forbes and his lone companion, lay helplessly at anchor in San Francisco harbor for over three months before the captain could get another crew.

By the end of May 1849, 59 vessels—17 of which were steamers—had disgorged almost 4,000 passengers at Chagres, all hellbent to get across the Isthmus and on to California. They represented most of the countries of the western world, but all those of the white race, regardless of their origins, were classified as "Yankees." During the decade of the 1850's thousands of these "Yankees" streamed back and forth across the Isthmus. Many became permanent residents, in the cemeteries of Chagres, Cruces, Gorgona and Panama City, and in unmarked graves on the jungle trail. They dominated the scene during this era, and their passage route between the Atlantic ports and Panama City on the Pacific became known as the Yankee Strip.

The Atlantic Terminus

THE VAST MIGRATION TO CALIFORNIA ASSURED THE FINANCIAL SUCcess of any railroad across the Isthmus, but, less happily, the rush would inevitably increase construction costs and make labor scarce. Prior to chartering the railroad corporation, Aspinwall petitioned the U. S. Congress to grant his company some sort of official recognition and a subsidy, so as to pay part of the cost and encourage private investors to purchase stock. The House Committee on Naval Affairs recommended an annual subsidy of $250,000 for mail transportation across the Isthmus "by any reliable means whatsoever," but no appropriation was made at that time.

In January 1849, Aspinwall hired Colonel George W. Hughes of the U. S. Army Topographical Corps to lead a group of engineers in making roadbed surveys on the Isthmus. Hughes, a West Pointer in his early forties, had served with distinction in the Mexican War on the staff of General Wool and as military governor of Jalapa. He was a competent civil engineer, but at times his better judgment was undermined by a desire to tell his employers what they wanted to hear. His group included the civilian engineer James L. Baldwin who had gone to the Isthmus the year before. Taking advantage of the dry season, the 38-man Hughes party ran lines for a roadbed 47¾ miles long from Navy Bay on the Caribbean to Panama City on the Pacific. Baldwin and Captain John J. Williams found a pass in the Continental Divide at Culebra 263 feet above sea level. Hughes believed that this notch could be deepened and thus reduce even further the maximum elevation of the roadbed.

In April 1849, while waiting for the survey to be completed, Aspinwall incorporated the Panama Railroad Company in the State of New York. John L. Stephens became president of the company and Colonel Alexander J. Center, vice president. The board of directors included William H. Aspinwall, James Brown, Cornelius Van Wyck Lawrence, Joseph B. Varnum, Samuel S. Howland, Prosper M. Wetmore, Edwin Bartlett and Horatio Allen. Several members of the board of directors of the Pacific Mail Steamship Company were also directors of the railroad, but the two corporations were nominally separate. The corporation charter authorized the company to sell $5,000,000 in stock, but the first subscription, issued in June 1849, attempted to raise only $1,000,000. Barely half of this subscription was purchased by the public at this first offering, so the directors had to buy the remainder. Then, with the company formed and stock issued, the directors urged Hughes to hasten in completing his survey.

On board the steamer *Crescent City* en route to New York during the first part of June, Colonel Hughes scribbled his report to the directors. The report was exceedingly optimistic and tended to minimize the seriousness of construction problems. Important parts of it later proved to be inaccurate. Hughes' line of survey ran south from Navy Bay on the Caribbean to the Chagres, then up the valley of the Chagres without crossing the river until it came to a spot about a mile from Gorgona where a large bridge was projected. The line then ran to Gatun, where another bridge would be necessary. Hughes said constructing these bridges presented no foreseeable difficulty in that they would not be nearly so large as many bridges built regularly in the United States. He suggested offhandedly that if the notch in the Continental Divide was not low enough, the ridge between Mandingo and Obispo could be pierced with a tunnel 1,400 feet long, a statement typical of his excessive optimism.

Hughes described the common soil of the Isthmus as "red clay and traprock," and neglected to mention the vast swamps and gelatinous savannas.

"Lumber of excellent quality is abundant," he wrote, perpetrating a misleading half-truth. It was true that certain heavy woods, such as mahogany and oak, were abundant. But the mahogany was scattered widely throughout dense forests of worthless trees, and the oak groves were isolated high in the mountains. Because of the scattering and the isolation of good timber, the cost of using native wood would prove much higher than importing it.

Hughes described the harbor of Navy Bay—which he envisioned as the Atlantic terminus—as "excellent" and stated unequivocably, "no breakwater is necessary to protect the shipping lying therein. A breakwater would be superfluous." Until the "superfluous" breakwater was built from Toro Point during the canal-digging days 60 years later, storms frequently roared into Navy Bay, foundering the anchored ships and ripping out large sections of wharf from the unprotected shore.

Hughes also said, "On the question of health, I consider the adverse accounts . . . much exaggerated; such of the inhabitants as live here *in the manner of human beings* enjoy as good health as people of the north, and of the great numbers of emigrants who have passed over during the present season, but few have suffered from local diseases." It might be noted that Hughes arrived on the Isthmus in late January and departed in early June, before the rains set in. He was thus spared the annual siege of malaria and dysentery characteristic of the rainy season.

Hughes estimated the construction cost of a single-track railroad across the Isthmus at $3,000,000, with additional harbor improvements at $1,500,000. But in commenting upon the possibility of digging a canal across the Isthmus, Hughes was gloomy, "unless the consideration of cost be disregarded." He felt compelled to increase greatly all previous estimates of this figure. "It will not be very extravagant to place it at . . . $50,000,000." (When the Panama Canal construction account was finally closed in 1921, a total of $386,910,301.04 had been spent.)

Captain Edward W. Serrell of the Hughes party took an even dimmer view of the possibility of a Panama canal. "The very considerable length through the base of the water-shed . . . together with the fact that no adequate sources exist for the supply of [water to] a summit level and lockages . . . must forever preclude the possibility of connecting the two oceans at this point by water communication."

Matthew Fontaine Maury, the famous oceanographer, then Superintendent of the U. S. Naval Observatory, disagreed with the notion that a Panama canal was out of the question or even far in the future. "The railroad across the Isthmus of Panama will speedily lead to the construction of a ship canal between the two oceans, for a railroad cannot do the business which commerce will require for it; and by showing to the world how immense this business is, men will come from the four quarters to urge with purse and tongue the construction of a ship canal." Maury was wrong only in his time concept, that construction of a railroad would "*speedily* lead to the construction of a ship canal." Events later proved that the railroad was vitally important to digging the canal in the twentieth century, but the means of digging the canal, even with a railroad, were simply not available in the nineteenth century.

The Executive Committee of the Panama Railroad Company met for the first time on July 9, 1849, in the railroad company office at 78 Broadway, New York City, and decided to meet regularly at 11 a.m. on Mondays, Wednesdays and Fridays. At the second meeting, on July 11, the committee designated Mr. Aspinwall responsible for the purchase of the iron rails and authorized the following advertisement placed in leading New York newspapers under the heading, "Notice to Railroad Contractors":

"On the first day of September next the Company will be ready to receive proposals, to be decided on as soon thereafter as possible, for grading and constructing a portion of the railroad across the Isthmus of Panama, viz. from the Chagres River to the terminus on the Pacific, being about twenty miles. This notice is given in advance in order that persons wishing to contract may have an opportunity of visiting the Isthmus and examining the line of road as staked out by the Corps of Engineers."

During August, as an aid to contractors in submitting bids, the company put on display at the railroad office the maps, plans and profiles prepared by Colonel Hughes, as well as an outline of building specifications. When serious interest among bidders still lagged, the committee ordered the following advertisement placed:

"In order to enable the contractors who may be disposed to visit the Isthmus of Panama by the *Empire City* which leaves on the 10th instant, the time for receiving proposals for the construction of the railroad will be extended to the first of October next. A competent person will be sent out by the company to point out the line of the road."

The crowded steamer *Empire City* sailed for the Isthmus with 20 interested contractors among its passengers. They made the bungo journey up the Chagres and rode the skinny mules down the tortuous road to the Pacific. While frantic gold-seekers rushed across with scarcely a glance around, these hardheaded men of business carefully considered the lay of the land, stopping frequently to take sightings with telescopes and to make notes. They dug samples of the earth, crushed it in their hands and smelled it. They cut limbs from trees to study the grain of the wood. On the return voyage to New York there were whispered conferences among partners with dubious head shakings and more scribbling of figures. All proposals were in by October 1. On October 12 the company announced that the firm of Totten and Trautwine had won the contract.

The Panama Railroad was fortunate in its contractors. George Muirson Totten, generally referred to as "Colonel" Totten even though he had no military rank, was a Connecticut Yankee then 41 years old, slight in stature, quiet and reserved in manner, with a luxuriant beard. At the age of 20 he started in canal building, working successively as an engineer in the construction of the Farmington, the Juniata and the Delaware and Raritan Canals. Entering railroad construction in 1835, ten years after the first experimental operation of a steam locomotive in the United States, he helped build railroads in Pennsylvania from Reading to Port Clinton and from Sunbury to Danville. From 1840 to 1843 he was chief construction engineer on the road connecting Gastonia and Raleigh, North Carolina.

His partner, John Cresson Trautwine of Philadelphia, was a year younger and perhaps better known in the engineering profession than Totten. Trautwine was the author of a handbook for civil engineers that is still in use today in a revised form. He was a recognized expert in railroad construction; the *Journal of the Franklin Institute* had published articles by him on such subjects as "the use of pilings in railroad superstructures," and "the injudicious policy pursued in the construction and machinery of many railroads in the United States."

Totten and Trautwine had had wide experience in Latin America, having worked a five-year contract, from 1843 to 1848, for the government of New Granada, dredging and widening the channel of the Canal del Dique, the waterway connecting the Magdalena River with the harbor of Cartagena. Their success in this project had earned them the confidence of the government at Bogotá as well as a large sum of money.

The two partners arrived on the Isthmus in October 1849 with the intention of beginning construction at Gorgona and building toward the Pacific. The Hughes survey had stated positively that the river was navigable to Gorgona by shallow-draft steamboats which could transport the necessary men, construction materials and supplies upriver. The railroad company sent down a specially designed steamer, the *General Herran,* to take over river service.

This craft could successfully ascend the river to Gorgona during the wet season, but the wood-eating teredo worms riddled its hull so thoroughly that within a few months the ship had to be towed to New Orleans for repairs. To thwart the predatory worms, the company sent down an iron-hulled steamer, the *Raphael Rivas.* The specifications of the vessel called for a 12-inch draft. However, 12 inches had been the draft of the *Rivas* before the iron sides were bolted on. The additional weight made her draw 30 inches and she was unable to get upriver beyond Palenquilla, 11 miles below Gorgona. Of course, the bungo boats could make the upriver trip even during the dry season, but they were too small to carry heavy equipment, and were so busy transporting gold-seekers across the Isthmus that their rates were prohibitive.

Regretfully, Totten and Trautwine petitioned for release from the building contract, suggesting that the company take direct charge of construction and that work begin on the Atlantic side of the Isthmus so that the railroad could carry its own equipment inland as the line was built. In November of 1849 the railroad company accepted the withdrawal of Totten and Trautwine as contractors, but hired them to build the road under company supervision.

From the first Trautwine had disagreed with many of the findings and recommendations of the Hughes survey. Now he disagreed with Hughes' plan to locate the Atlantic terminus at Navy Bay. The land was too marshy there, Trautwine said, and also the harbor was dangerous in bad weather unless an expensive breakwater was constructed. Trautwine suggested that the terminus be Porto Bello, 20 miles east of Navy Bay, or somewhere on the coast between the two points. Colonel G. W. Hughes bristled at the idea. The colonel was presently serving as Chief Engineer of the railroad company, a position won largely by his work on the initial survey. He had stated on the record that a breakwater at Navy Bay was superfluous. Hughes now pointed out to the board that Porto Bello was several miles farther from Panama City than was Navy Bay, and that to make it a terminus would add greatly to the estimated construction costs. Trautwine's differences with the chief engineer over the terminus caused dissension among the members of the board of directors. While this argument raged, George Law became indirectly responsible for the final selection of the site.

As owner of the United States Mail Steam Line, Law had hitherto been acclaimed as the most astute financier in the United States because his franchise had captured the wealthy, populous cities of the Eastern Seaboard—New York, Charleston, Savannah and New Orleans. But now, with the vast migration of the Gold Rush sweeping passengers and freight westward, the Aspinwall coup in negotiating the exclusive concession on the Isthmus overshadowed him. Law decided to pull off a coup of his own and extort for himself a block of Panama Railroad stock and a seat on the board of directors.

George Law secretly dispatched a confidential agent, "Colonel" Albert Zwingle, to the Isthmus. Zwingle had engaged in several filibustering expeditions in Central America, spoke fluent Spanish, and had a nice command of the intrigue and double-dealing necessary to doing business successfully there. He arrived in Porto Bello with a carpetbag full of Yankee currency and within a day or two had bought options on all the water-front land between Porto Bello and the far end of Navy Bay. Thus his employer George Law was able to confront the Panama Railroad Company with a monopoly on the water-front land at the most favorable locations for the Atlantic terminus. Law demanded a huge block of railroad stock for the land as well as membership on the board of directors.

At a hastily called meeting the railroad directors scanned maps and wrangled. The only public land available for the Atlantic terminus was Manzanillo Island, which lay just offshore from Black Swamp. Using the island would necessitate building a causeway across the intervening strip of water to the mainland, and then laying trackage across 3,000 yards of swampland. But the land would cost nothing. The directors decided to reject Law's offer and gamble on using Manzanillo. They had no conception of the terrible hardships they were creating for their building contractors in making this decision. But the decision was made. After work began, and the railroad was definitely committed to begin on Manzanillo, Law let his options lapse, suffering a considerable financial loss in the process. But he was not discouraged. The following year he purchased $300,000 of Panama Railroad stock and for years exerted a strong influence on the company, although he never became a member of the board of directors.

On a May morning in 1850, John C. Trautwine and James L. Baldwin chartered half a dozen bungo boats at Chagres and paddled down the coast to Manzanillo. Totten was in Cartagena recruiting labor, leaving his partner in charge. Trautwine and Baldwin had with them a dozen natives armed with machetes and axes. They stepped ashore on the coral rim of Manzanillo and stared across the 650 sunken acres of the island. Manzanillo had originally been a sand bar. "Upon these bars," Trautwine explained, "floating trees and logs are lodged and retained, and by constant accumulation soon reach the surface, when vegetation commences and progresses with great rapidity."

Clouds of buzzing mosquitoes swarmed around each man, stinging faces, necks and backs of hands. Slapping away at the insects, the white men, followed by their lethargic native helpers, gloomily walked along the sandy beach, looking across the channel to the mainland. This channel, which no longer exists, ran east and west and was about 200 yards wide. Toward the east it broadened as it merged into Manzanillo Bay. There the surface of the water revealed a cluster of a dozen or so small islands, gradually developing in the same manner as had Manzanillo. Westward, the channel widened into a placid basin, separated by a narrow belt of water foliage from the large expanse of Navy Bay. The waters of the channel were constantly broken by leaping fish, called "flores del mar" by the natives because of their brilliant colors.

The mainland shore—the Black Swamp—was walled with a barrier of mangrove. In the manner of their growth, these mangrove bushes resembled banyan trees. Their branches first grew upward and then bent downward to enter the soil and take root themselves, entwining into a formidable barrier which would yield only to axes or machetes. Many of the mangrove branches dipping into the water were covered with oyster-like mollusks, varying in size from that of a dime to a silver dollar, and highly esteemed as food by the natives.

Behind the barrier lay the swamp itself, formed by the flowing together of several rivers and creeks just before reaching the sea. Trautwine, exploring the area on foot and by bungo, was amazed at the number of streams involved and the instability of the soil.

"At the immediate banks of the streams," he wrote, "the swamps are elevated a few inches above the water-surface . . . but at the distance of a few rods back they are about level with it; consequently, when the rivers are swelled a foot or two, by either a rise of the river above, or by the action of the . . . winds in forcing the salt water of the gulf inland, this broad expanse of marsh becomes inundated; presenting the appearance of an immense lake studded with trees.

"The soil is composed of a black mud and very fine sand, which supports a vegetation of undergrowth and trees; generally dense near the water's edge, but more sparse at some distance back from it. I observed that none of the trees attained more than a very moderate size. That is, probably, attributable, in part, to the effect of the salt and fresh water, in which their roots are alternately submerged; for, above the point to which the water of the gulf is sometimes driven, the trees are larger."

The interior of Manzanillo, the platform from which the railroad was to spring across the channel, was similar in appearance to the mainland, according to Dr. F. N. Otis, the first historian of the Panama Railroad.

"It was a virgin swamp, covered with a dense growth of the tortuous, water-loving mangrove, and interlaced with huge vines and thorny shrubs, defying entrance to the wild beasts common to the country. In the black, slimy mud of its surface alligators and other reptiles abounded; while the air was laden with pestilential vapors, and swarming with sand-flies and mosquitoes. These last proved so annoying to the laborers that, unless their faces were protected by gauze veils, no work could be done, even at midday."

The ground-breaking for the railroad was neither pretentious nor ceremonial. Trautwine and Baldwin, knee-deep in the stagnant water, swung their axes at the trunk of a cocoa palm, their blows ringing clear and sharp in the muggy heat. The tall palm teetered and fell with a splash into the waters of the bay. Construction had begun on the Panama Railroad from the Atlantic terminus on Manzanillo Island. Other than the natives, the only spectators were gawky pelicans which flapped laboriously into the air when the strange hubbub began, and alligators, soaking in the ooze, which pushed off into the water to watch proceedings from a safe distance.

IV

The Golden Chimera

THE CHEST OF GOLD DISPLAYED AT THE WAR OFFICE IN WASHINGTON proved to be a Pandora's Box, scattering the germs of delirium far and wide. Gold fever. It swept from Maine to the Gulf Coast with fantastic speed for that era of slow communications. Even in calm, cautious New England the native skepticism quickly turned into abject credulity. Any tale of California gold, no matter how preposterous, was swallowed whole. People believed that nuggets clustered themselves about shallow grass roots awaiting the harvester. They believed that mountain streams gleamed bright yellow because the water flowed over beds of flake gold several feet thick. They believed that Indians sought out white men, offering sacks of nuggets in exchange for cheap, shiny gewgaws, and that a bottle of whiskey could buy a pound of gold dust from any savage. Vast numbers of Americans who had never known anything but hard work and coarse fare now saw a quick way to wealth and luxury. Gold fever.

No section of the country was spared. Mechanics dropped their tools, students their books; clerks left their counters and judges their benches—all to join the Gold Rush. Impatience was their most noticeable characteristic. Even the vast stores of gold in California must have a limit somewhere—there could not possibly be enough to make *everybody* rich. You had to get there first, grab your share of the treasure, and then sit back and smile at the laggards who arrived too late. But now you must hurry. You must rush to California.

In many communities the exodus of men slowed agriculture, manufacturing and trade almost to a standstill. This could not be tolerated. *Somebody* had to stay home. Preachers sermonized on the pitfalls that lay in the path of the suddenly wealthy. Editors urged young men who had not yet taken the irrevocable step, "to observe well the men who have attained security and useful careers in their own communities, and weigh the advantages of slow, sure gains at home against the perils of the dangerous and expensive journey to California."

These admonitions from the pulpit and the press, however, were generally made for the benefit of someone other than he who uttered them. One young man who lagged behind in an agony of indecision created by preachers and editorialists finally saw the light and said, "Ministers who had prophesied unutterable woes upon the country started on the first ship available as missionaries. Editors who in the columns of their papers had discouraged the movement sold out and by virtue of their character as representatives of the press obtained extraordinary facilities for transportation and anticipated the quickest of us by at least a month."

General economic conditions in 1849 favored a susceptibility to get-rich-quick adventures. A period of business depression had followed the Mexican War, increasing the number of the jobless. Thousands of ex-soldiers, idle and restless, were ready for any scheme that promised wealth and adventure. Also, the entire Eastern Seaboard was overshadowed by a fear of death. That summer cholera struck in epidemic proportions. For two months the disease killed over 700 people a week in New York City alone. Better to gamble, then, on sudden wealth or a hero's death on the way to California than on poverty and an ignominious puking demise by cholera in the East.

Two general routes led to the gold fields. One was overland across the continent, a long, hard journey imperiled by Indians on the plains and blizzards in the mountains. The other was by ship around Cape Horn or to one of the narrower sections of the continental barrier and across to the opposite sea. Those with money enough to buy speed chose ship travel.

All of the sea routes to the gold fields were crowded in 1849. As fast as United States vessels returned to their home ports from abroad, they were put on the California run. Ships flying the Stars and Stripes virtually disappeared from the harbors of the world outside of Central and South America. New England's large whaling fleet, converted almost completely to passenger service, went southward around the Horn loaded with gold hunters instead of harpoonists. Eastern shipyards worked around the clock rushing to completion vessels of all kinds—especially steamers. The ship shortage remained acute for several years. Speculators, digging their gold in the East, ransacked ports and harbors for any floatable hulk. Dozens of rotting, long-abandoned craft were pulled from mud banks, patched up and sent to sea loaded with passengers. Many a ship broker prayed only that his latest reconditioned tub get out of sight of land, before sinking. That way it would take months for the relatives to verify the deaths of loved ones and by then the ship broker would have made his fortune and disappeared.

George Law's United States Mail Steam Line advertised the advantages of the Panama crossing in newspapers and handbills. By making the right connections at Panama it was possible to travel from New York City to San Francisco in six weeks. Law's steamers carried most of the Argonauts—the New York *Herald Tribune's* name for sea travelers to California—on the voyage to Panama. The ships left New York at 2 p.m. on the 5th and 20th of each month from the Warren Street Pier on the North River. Ticket holders had to push their way through a crowd of draymen, hackmen, fruit-women, book peddlers, pitchmen, porters and beggars.

"Get your shovels here!" shouted the pitchmen selling tools. "Get your bellows! Everyone needs bellows! Pouches and belts to hold your gold!"

Farther from the dock other hucksters sold canned foods to travelers worried about a shortage of rations. These salesmen stayed back from the dock because the steamship companies objected to their wares. The canning of food was not an exact science in the 1850's; almost inevitably the cans exploded after a few days at sea, splattering cramped quarters with stinking goo. Sea captains who heard of canned goods on their ships invariably ordered them dumped overboard.

Because of the highly colored accounts of hardships on the Isthmus which appeared constantly in the New York newspapers, travelers could be induced to buy all sorts of absurd and useless articles for their own comfort: folding drinking cups which leaked but did not fold, pocket water filters to "purify" contaminated water, India rubber mattresses which could not be blown up, "cholera preventative," life preservers, and according to the traveler J. D. Borthwick, "every contrivance imaginable to protect precious persons against sun, wind and rain."

Other travelers, worried about obtaining boat and mule passage across the Isthmus, purchased tickets for the crossing from agents on the dock at New York. After taking their money, the agent handed them colorful tickets and told them to contact "Doc White" on board the ship and he would arrange for their Isthmian transport. Needless to say, these duped travelers could never locate Doc White.

Just before the steamship gangplank was raised, a light wagon drawn by snorting, prancing horses dashed recklessly through the crowd, bringing the last express and the mails. Then, with smoke spouting blackly from the stacks, the steamer's large red paddle wheels began to turn and she headed downriver at 11 or 12 knots, past the Battery, Governor's and Bedloe's Islands, and finally

Staten Island, whose shores were then dotted with the summer villas of the well-to-do.

The ship's purser formed a line of crewmen with hands joined to walk down the deck, and began collecting tickets. In order to pass through this line, each passenger had to surrender his ticket and receive a claim check. Those without tickets were hustled to the hurricane deck and locked in a wire pen with chickens and other fowls. There they stood disconsolately amid the clucking and crowing of the doomed poultry, suffering the ridicule of the legitimate passengers. Some of the ticket holders themselves, however, were in for unpleasant surprises, finding that their "forward cabin" tickets, purchased from cut-rate dealers, meant "steerage" in reality. These swindled bargain hunters were sent below, where a crude society greeted them with jeers and catcalls.

When the steam launch appeared off Sandy Hook to pick up the harbor pilot, the stowaways from the chicken pen were shoved down the gangway by hardhanded mates and crewmen. As the steamer turned south, carrying its load of passengers toward their golden dreams, the losers returned to shore in the pilot boat scheming to steal passage money or stow away on another ship.

On the southward voyage, the Argonauts sprawled about on their piles of gear: reading, writing letters, gambling with cards and dice, or just staring into space dreaming of gold. They came from all walks of life. Gentlemen in silk hats, stock collars and Inverness capes lounged next to sallow-faced mountaineers in jeans pants and grimy buckskin shirts. They were mostly young men, away from home and family for the first time. Their moods vacillated hourly from the height of exaltation—they would strike it rich for sure—to the abyss of despair—the gold would all be gone by the time they got there. In a breath they ranged from vast plans for spending large fortunes to somber considerations of what to say if they returned home in rags.

The correspondence of young Daniel A. Horn of Alabama, who traveled by steamer to the Isthmus in 1849, projects these contrasting moods. After writing home from New Orleans of his absolute certainty of success in the gold fields, he followed with a reflective shipboard letter two days later saying in part, ". . . as soon as I am satisfied I cannot do well, I will return home, despite the scoffs that may be thrown at me."

Many of the travelers were haunted by thoughts of death, especially the deaths of loved ones which might occur during their absences. A religious note marked their expressions of anxiety. Young Horn wrote, "It is my greatest fear that my dear mother or some member of my family may be taken away so that I will never see them again in this life, but may God grant that we may meet in the 'Home of pure delight where Saints immortal dwell.'"

To ward off loneliness and promote efficiency many gold-seekers traveled in organized groups bound together by codes of regulations drawn up prior to departure. They elected leaders and some devised uniforms which gave them a quasi-military appearance. Many of these groups were quite informal, but others were incorporated joint-stock companies. During 1849 over 100 incorporated companies sailed from Massachusetts alone. Each member paid an equal sum into the treasury and each had an equal vote in its management and expected to share equally in the profits. Some groups had bylaws prohibiting such vices as gambling, drinking and swearing, with prescribed punishments for violators. Many of the rules expressed the general optimism of the travelers. For example, a rule of one group provided that should the amount of gold they gathered so overburden their ship as to make her dangerous to sail on the homeward voyage, then part of the treasure had to be left behind, under guard, until means were found of getting it home safely.

Many of the groups, organized and financed by businessmen who remained at home, took along merchandise for sale in California. "Even if we fail to dig an ounce of gold," wrote a member of a company traveling on the schooner *Roanoke*, "the supplies we are bringing out with us will return each of us a sum larger than we could have earned at home." Of course most of the companies carrying trade goods made the entire journey by sea, around the Horn, to eliminate the expensive Panama transit.

Julius H. Pratt, a 27-year-old New England businessman, organized such a company in 1849. "Twenty good men, who subscribed to a code of laws for associate government and to articles of agreement for two years service," was Pratt's description. Each put up $500 cash to make a total capital of $10,000. They also bought uniforms—"short gray single-breasted frock coats with gilt eagle buttons and shiny black forage caps"—as well as armament —"a carbine, a revolver and a Bowie knife." In addition, each carried 75 pounds of clothing and bedding packed in watertight rubber bags. A doctor was recruited as a member, with the stipulation he furnish a medical chest and surgical instruments. Books of sermons were taken as a substitute for a chaplain. "The books may be read to great religious advantage and still not consume rations on workdays," said Pratt.

Church services were held at home prior to the departure of Pratt's group. The text of the sermon was from the 28th Chapter of Job—"Surely there is a vein for the silver and a place for the gold where they fine it." It is a credit to Pratt and his organization that on their journey to California—which took almost four months because of delays at Panama on the coast of Mexico—they did not lose a single man.

The Argonauts were all armed and tooled to the teeth. Brandishing Slakin's six-barreled pistols, Colt and Allen revolvers and Jenk's patent carbines and rifles, they also carried picks, shovels, axes, strange gold-washing machines and steel retorts for melting the gold dust into bars. Optimistically, they lugged about huge money belts and wooden chests to transport their treasure home from the gold fields.

Women joined the sea migration to California in increasing numbers. Their presence was commented upon by several sensitive male observers.

The historian Hubert H. Bancroft, looking back on his voyage, said, "Gamblers, braggarts and brazen-faced young women made life difficult for sober-minded travelers. They seemed to vie with each other in rendering themselves disagreeably conspicuous."

At night the first-class passengers could retire to their staterooms, or if the weather was clear, stand about on the upper deck. The staterooms were tiny and crowded with four berths, washstand, mirror and baggage rack. A porthole admitted light and air, but the rooms were often stifling hot in the tropics, especially those near the engine room or boilers.

To one male imbued with Victorian standards, the situation at night on the open deck was positively shocking. "Although it is very dark, you will observe that the benches around the ship's rail are filled with human beings. You will see as you inspect these benches females in the close embrace of those of the sterner sex, their heads reclining in the most loving manner on the shoulders of their male protectors. You will naturally enough suppose them to be husband and wife or sister and brother. They are in some cases, but more frequently are not. Generally speaking they are only a couple whose acquaintance dates back to the ship's sailing!"

The dark, crowded quarters of the steerage, deep in the ship, were filled from floor to ceiling with tiers of berths. Here, in a noisy confusion totally lacking in privacy, men, women and children were thrown together with no segregation as to sex whatsoever. Females in the steerage acted in a manner even more appalling than their sisters on deck, according to the same persistent moralizer who had surveyed the deck scene at night. His investigation in the steerage inspired this description in his journal:

"Directly at the foot of the steps, lying on her back, is an Irish woman weighing not less than two hundred and fifty pounds. She is almost without clothing, so great is the heat. . . . Women can be seen in this cabin who have apparently lost all sense of decency, who at home would cover the legs of a piano, so particular were they in regard to anything appearing naked."

But the voyage was not all shock and unpleasantness, even to the most sensitive, especially if the weather was clear. The ships generally stayed close to shore, and the passengers could loll under awnings watching a changing panorama of palm-lined coasts, rolling green hills and distant mountains. A spirit of sociability then enlivened the ship. Bancroft says, "Gossips took heart; matrons smiled serenely; paterfamilias grew jocund; attention turned toward comfort, reading and amusements. Gallants mixed huge pitchers of iced punch, and therewith regaled the ladies. . . ."

Despite these periods of conviviality, time passed slowly. The passengers sought distraction. During 1849 and 1850 professional gamblers rode all the ships, spreading out faro and roulette games on the dining room tables. Later, when gambling was officially prohibited by the steamship companies because of the large number of women and children among the passengers, card and dice games went on in staterooms. Bancroft observed that other wagering was constant, "on daily distances, on the time of arrival at any point, on the height or weight of any person or thing, on the time in which coat and boots could be taken off and put on, and on anything that happened to strike the fancy, however absurd."

The lethargy of the voyage was broken twice a day by the sudden clang of the dinner bell and the thundering rush of passengers to the dining saloon. The sight of food brought out the beast in the passengers, both men and women. They pushed, shoved and wrestled for places at the long table and snatched chunks of bread and meat from each other. The food—platters of potatoes, boiled beef, biscuits, beans and sea pie—was of poor quality and barely cooked. On each table was a tublike bowl filled with a blackish hash which the Argonauts called lobscouse.

One traveler, Ezekiel I. Barra, related a ship's cook's recipe for the lobscouse: ". . . one onion cut and put into a gallon of water, a dozen potatoes peeled and cut into quarters, four cakes of navy bread soaked and broken up. Boil for an hour. Cut up salt pork into small square pieces equal to one third of the whole mass, and boil all again for half an hour. Then add pepper to taste, and add, when it is about to be taken up, a half cupful of thickening."

Barra, whose journal dwells on food at great length, also included this recipe for sea pie:

"A sea pie consists of onions fried brown, lean pork cut in small pieces, potatoes cut in quarters, and then all simmered together;

then make dough enough to cover the sides of a baking pan and put in the filling of stew, season with tomato ketchup and pepper, spring in a little flour to thicken it, and cover the pan with a thick crust and put it in the oven for two hours."

According to Barra, the dessert at every meal was either dandyfunk or plum duff.

"Dandyfunk is a dish composed of navy biscuit soaked in water, mashed with a pestle, mixed with fat taken from the coppers in which the meat is boiled, sweetened with molasses and flavored with allspice, then put into a pan and baked in the oven. It isn't a very high-toned dish, but in the absence of something better is very palatable to a sailor.

"Plum duff is composed of flour, lard, raisins and saleratus, with eggs mixed in when they can be had. When well mixed it is put into a canvas bag, wide at the top and very narrow at the bottom, boiled for two hours and then turned out into a platter and served with wine sauce when it can be had, or else with vinegar, butter, sugar and water boiled well together and thickened with flour and flavored with nutmeg."

With such a diet, the eventual approach to the Isthmus was doubly welcome. The first sight of Panama was the headland of Porto Bello, described by Bayard Taylor, the author from Pennsylvania, as "a bold, rocky promontory, fringed with vegetation and washed at its foot by a line of snowy breakers." Far in the distance the travelers could see the towering Andes reaching up into the clouds. Turning west, the steamer passed Navy Bay, discovered by Columbus in 1502, where construction of the Panama Railroad was now beginning. Eight miles farther along the coast they came to the mouth of the Chagres.

Long before the ship dropped anchor the deck was covered with piles of luggage brought up from below by pushing, shoving passengers, all anxious to be first to disembark. Ignoring the tumult, the ship's purser roughly forced his way across the deck and went ashore in the lighter to send forward the mail and insured express. The number of boats available at Chagres for the river trip fluctuated greatly, and the purser wanted to take care of his own business first.

"It was amusing," said J. M. Letts, who arrived at Chagres on the *Marietta* in early 1849, "to see the passengers preparing to make their advent to land. It is well understood that no one started for California without being thoroughly fortified, and as we had arrived at a place, where, as we thought, there must be at least *some* fighting to do, our first attention was directed to our *armor*. The revolvers, each man having at least two, were first overhauled, and the six barrels charged. These were put in our belt, which also contained a bowie knife. A brace of smaller pistols were snugly pocketed inside our vest; our rifles were liberally charged; and with a cane in hand (which of course contains a dirk), and a *sling shot* in our pockets, we wait impatiently to step off and look around for the enemy."

On his return "the purser was assailed by such a storm of questions—the passengers leaning half-way out over the bulwarks—that he could not make himself heard," Taylor said. When the noise had quieted, the purser told them when the next steamer would sail from Panama City—or when it was *supposed* to sail—and then announced that no one could go ashore until next morning. The passengers took most of their gear below again, grumbling, trying to resign themselves to another night wasted on the ship while their treasure was being stolen by others in California. The more impatient ones refused to go below and slept on their piled-up gear, determined to be among the first ashore next morning. During the long night those on deck were diverted by lightning storms flashing and crackling over the shoreline. Taylor was fascinated by "the broad, scarlet flashes of lightning, surpassing any celestial pyrotechnics I ever witnessed. The dark walls of San Lorenzo, the brilliant clusters of palms on the shore, and the green, rolling hills of the interior at intervals leaped starkly out of the gloom."

Many of the deck-sleepers, not at all entertained by the storm, scurried below. It was then preached in many churches that lightning was the instrument sent by a wrathful God to strike down sinners. There were those who, unnerved by memories of past transgressions, did not wish to tempt the Almighty by remaining exposed on deck.

At dawn they went ashore in the lighters, "rounding the high bluff on which the castle stands and finding beyond it a shallow little bay on the eastern shore of which, on low ground, stand the cane huts of Chagres." After the boats were grounded on the sand, the Argonauts splashed through the shallows to the beach.

The boatmen charged two dollars to land each passenger and his baggage. In stormy weather the fee was well earned, for the larger steamers did not dare come close to the treacherous river mouth, where the rocks and sand bar had wrecked four of Morgan's ships during a storm in 1670 and, more recently, several steamers. Sometimes the steamers had to anchor off Chagres for days, pitching and rolling, waiting for the turbulent sea to settle. Occasionally the lighter crews, spurred on by the reckless bids of the impatient passengers, put their boats into the rough sea and were swamped, drowning everyone aboard.

When the first contingent of gold-seekers, those from the *Falcon* in December 1848, arrived at Chagres, they found that none of the populace had heard of the gold strike. The 212 Americans tried vainly to communicate their urgent need for transportation upriver to the lethargic natives, who understood only a bastard Spanish or African dialect. Finally, the Americans lost patience and with drawn guns forced the reluctant natives to their boats. Some of the boatmen cast off with pistols against their heads. The first group paid a dollar apiece for the trip to Cruces, but the fare was never that low again. The price zoomed to $15, or more. Sometimes the boatmen could not be prevailed upon to work at any price because they wanted to attend a fiesta or a cockfight.

The natives of Chagres, said the traveler E. S. Capron, were mainly Negroes and Indians. Some, by intermarriage with whites, had produced a breed having "a few of the good and many of the bad qualities of both races. Ignorance, treachery, dishonesty, cowardice, and indolence are universal characteristics. The devotion to gambling amounts to perfect mania."

Almost without exception the travelers were critical of the Isthmian inhabitants. Theodore T. Johnson, arriving at Chagres on the *Crescent City* in February 1849, was appalled by the huddle of bamboo huts, its muddy streets "filled with a confused mixture of dogs, hogs and naked children, Negroes and Creoles." Johnson reported that his fellow-passengers, incensed by the indolence of the native boatmen, took up the cry: "Whip the rascal, fire his den, burn the settlement, annex the Isthmus!" All of which—actions and words—helped create the native antagonism toward Yankees which exploded into the bloody riots of the future.

The animosity of the Argonauts toward the Isthmian population stemmed mostly from their demonic desire for speed, to get across ahead of those coming behind them. Emotions were heightened by meetings with successful miners, traveling across the Isthmus eastward, homeward-bound with fortunes from the gold diggings. Bayard Taylor encountered such a traveler soon after his arrival at Chagres:

"A returning Californian had just reached the place, with a box containing $22,000 in gold dust, and a four-pound lump in one hand. The impatience and excitement of the passengers, already at high pitch, was greatly increased by his appearance. Life and death were small matters compared with immediate departure from Chagres. Men ran up and down the beach, shouting, gesticulating, and getting feverishly impatient at the deliberate habits of the natives; as if their arrival in California would thereby be at all hastened. The boatmen, knowing very well that two or more steamers were due the next day, remained provokingly cool and unconcerned. They had not seen six months of emigration without learning something of the American habit of going at full speed."

V

The Rise of the Derienni

IN JANUARY 1849, THE ARRIVAL OF THE HUGHES GROUP TO SURVEY the railroad line had led to the creation of the new town of "Yankee Chagres" on the shore of the river opposite the old town of "native" Chagres. The town's beginning was a wharf built by the railroad company, where the small steamer *Orus* could dock and unload supplies for the survey party. A prefabricated building of Georgia pine, sent down on the *Orus,* was placed on the dock as a tool shed. It was the first building in Yankee Chagres. As the number of gold-seekers increased, additional wharves were developed along the shore. The jungle was cut back and two more crude buildings of Georgia pine—called hotels—were built. A shantytown mushroomed around the hotels—frame shacks, tents, lean-tos and bamboo huts—housing saloons, gambling houses and brothels. These establishments were operated by American and European entrepreneurs for the entertainment of the Argonauts.

Joseph W. Gregory's *Guide For California Travellers Via The Isthmus Of Panama,* published in 1850, lists the principal hotels of Yankee Chagres as the Irvine House, the Californian and the

Crescent City. The hotels were unpainted two-story structures with wide porches circling both floors. Their rooms were filled with cots renting for four dollars a night. During crowded periods hammocks were swung from posts on the porches and between the cots. Generally one room was reserved for women and small children, but if the demand for beds was too great, the hotel keepers put men and women in the same rooms and made a meager attempt to screen off the women's cots with partitions of palm matting or bed sheets.

In addition to the hotel dining rooms, the Eagle Cafe and Restaurant, and a shanty with a cookstove and two long bare tables, called "Joe Prince's," served food. The fare, from all accounts, was terrible. Thin strips of beef cut several yards long and dried in the sun—called jerked beef—were a staple, as were dried beans, hardtack, moldy bread, and coffee. Tropical fruits, coconuts and plantains were available to hardy travelers willing to risk flux from eating native food.

Drinking was widespread. All the hotels had barrooms and there were many individual saloons. Liquor that cost ten cents a drink in New York was a dollar a drink in the bars of Yankee Chagres, but the Argonauts willingly paid the price. After a ship's arrival, the saloons were crowded from early in the morning until late at night.

There was no sewage system and no cemetery. Corpses were thrown into the Chagres with other refuse, to be carried out to sea. But the Chagres, one of the most perverse of rivers, often failed to carry its burdens a sufficient distance. The refuse boiled around in the warm water of the offshore sand bar, and the sluggish breeze blowing from the sea returned to the town an appalling stink. When the breeze reversed itself and blew from the Black Swamp, it brought other trials—swarms of mosquitoes and cockroaches. The buildings were without screens of any sort, but to close the heavy shutters in the stifling heat made life inside intolerable.

Cash flowed into the town. Most of the travelers had plenty of money; otherwise they could not have afforded the expensive Isthmus route. The westbound travelers had their grubstakes and the ones returning home had struck it rich, or at least had made money, because prospectors unsuccessful at the diggings could afford only to straggle home overland. Some of the money went to hotel and saloon-keepers, but most of it went to the gambling houses which offered roulette, faro, blackjack, trente-et-quarante, casino, poker and craps. The minimum bet was two dollars and the sky was the limit.

Hostesses in the saloons took their share. They charged two dollars a dance—once around the room only, as their time was limited. When a customer bought a hostess a drink she ordered a "Blue Moon"—colored water. The Blue Moon cost a dollar, from which the girl received 50 cents. Most of the girls also worked as prostitutes in the House of All Nations or in small tents, selling themselves not at all cheaply. From the vice-ridden ports of New Orleans, Marseilles and Cartagena they had come, and those of the darker colors predominated.

Regardless of these diversions, it was not a town in which to linger, especially for the westward-bound passenger. But it was not always very easy to get out. To ascend the Chagres—the first leg of the journey across the Isthmus—bungo boats were used. These were crude canoes about 25 feet long and three feet wide, carved from single guayacan logs. Generally they had a canopy of palm leaves, called a "toldo," to protect the cargo of Yankees from the sun. Each bungo accommodated four to six passengers in addition to the two or three boatmen.

The distance from Chagres to Panama City by river and trail was about 60 miles. During the first year of the rush the trip across took about five days. The boat journey up the meandering Chagres consumed about two-thirds of the journey. The last third—a wretched 20 miles of trail—involved crossing the Continental Divide and descending the slope to the Pacific Coast. But most of the time, it seemed, was spent waiting for the natives to get moving.

"The great secret" of rapid transit up the river, advised Gregory, "is to get off early in the morning and be liberal to the men that work the canoe. You can coax better than drive them."

Once in motion the bungos glided upriver at ten to 12 miles

per day. The river wound crookedly between high hills covered with a dense green jungle of palm trees, vines, cane thickets and bright tropical flowers. The boatmen had to work strenuously against the current to steer around snags, sand bars and shallow rapids.

As they dipped their long oars in the water, the boatmen, glistening with sweat, chanted monotonous songs. Occasionally monkeys answered chattering from the jungle, or a jaguar yowled. When they grew tired the natives quarreled with each other and inevitably tried to put into the bank for siestas. The impatient Yankees under the toldos would draw their guns threateningly to make them continue.

During the day, the travelers talked or dozed in the heat, slapping at flies and mosquitoes. At night they stopped in villages on the river bank and slept in hammocks in native huts or on the lice-infested floor mats. Some pitched tents, while others, traveling light, rolled up in blankets under the stars.

Surprisingly, many of the travelers enjoyed themselves. "The voyage up the Chagres," said Gregory, "has been by some persons execrated in tolerably strong terms, not to say diabolical. As far as my own feelings were concerned, I never beheld more magnificent scenery, or luxuriant vegetation."

Bayard Taylor, an experienced traveler, called the river journey "decidedly more novel, grotesque and adventurous than any trip of similar length in the world." On landing at Chagres, Taylor and three friends paid $15 each to engage a boat to Cruces. Mindful of Gregory's "great secret" of the early start, they stood watchfully over the boatmen refitting the bungo and then helped push the boat through the mud and shoal water to the river bank. But, busying themselves with stowing their gear, they temporarily relaxed their surveillance. When they looked up, the natives had disappeared. Taylor and his companions had "to wait the pleasure of the dusky gondoliers while the sun blazed down on the swampy shores, and visions of yellow fever came to the minds of the more timid." Around noon their boatmen came back, each carrying a bag of rice, a chunk of dried pork and an armful of sugar cane stalks to serve as rations for the trip. "A few strokes of their broad paddles took us from the excitement of the landing-place to the seclusion and beauty of the river."

The chief boatman of the Taylor group was Ambrosio Mendez, a mestizo; his assistant was Juan Crispin Bega, a Negro; and an anonymous runaway soldier from the Colombian army who, after tearful supplication, was allowed to work his passage completed the crew. Scarcely out of sight of Chagres, the runaway soldier demanded five dollars a day for his labor. Taylor refused; the deserter stopped working. When Taylor ordered Ambrosio to turn into the shore so that the man could be forcibly put off the boat, the deserter began half-heartedly paddling again. Even so, Taylor and his companions determined to leave him at Gatun, later in the day.

Taylor then settled back to enjoy the scenery:

"There is nothing in the world comparable to these forests. No description conveys an idea of the splendid overplus of vegetable life. . . . The river, broad, and with a swift current of the sweetest water I ever drank, winds between walls of foliage that rise from its very surface. All the gorgeous growths of an eternal summer are mingled in one impenetrable mass so that the eye is bewildered. From the rank jungles of cane and gigantic lilies, and the thickets of strange shrubs which line the water, rise the trunks of the mango, the ceiba, the cocoa, the sycamore, and the superb palm. Plantains take root in the banks, hiding the soil with their leaves, shaken and split into immense plumes by wind and rain. The zapote, with a fruit the size of a man's head, the gourd tree, other wonders, attract the eye on all sides. Blossoms of crimson, purple, yellow, of forms and magnitude unknown in the north. . . . Flocks of paroquets, brilliant butterflies circle like blossoms blown away. . . . A spike of scarlet flowers thrusts from the heart of a convolution of unfolding leaves. . . . Creepers and parasites drop trains and streamers of fragrance from boughs that shoot halfway across the river. All outline of the landscape is lost under this deluge of vegetation. No trace of the soil is to be seen; lowland and highland are the same; a mountain is but a higher swell of the mass of verdure. The sharp, clear lines of our scenery at home are here wanting. What shape the land would be if cleared, you cannot tell. You gaze upon the scene before you with a never-sated delight, till your brain aches with the sensation, and you close your eyes, overwhelmed with the thought that these wonders have been here from the beginning, that year after year takes away no blossom or leaf that is not replaced, but the sublime mystery of growth and decay is renewed forever."

In the afternoon they reached Gatun and found all of the earlier boats tied up there. The boatmen, to the great frustration of their passengers, had decided to stay overnight. The deserter from the Colombian army passively refused to leave the boat, so Taylor and his friends picked him up bodily and tossed him ashore with his belongings. They engaged another boatman to finish the trip for eight dollars. "I shall never forget the forlorn look of the ousted man as he sat on the bank beside his bag of rice, as the rain began to fall," said Taylor.

At Gatun Taylor found space for the night in a native hut, "a single room, in which all of the household operations were carried on." He described the tribulations of these lodgings in detail:

"A notched pole, serving as a ladder, led to a sleeping loft, under the pyramidal roof of thatch. Here a number of the emigrants who arrived late were stowed away on a rattling floor of cane, covered with hides. After a supper of pork and coffee, I made my day's notes by the light of a miserable starveling candle, stuck in an empty bottle, but had not written far before my paper was covered with fleas. The owner of the hut swung my hammock meanwhile, and I turned in to secure it for the night. To lie there was one thing, to sleep another. A dozen natives crowded round the table, drinking their aguardiente and disputing vehemently; the cooking fire was on one side of me, and every one who passed to and fro was sure to give me a thump, while my weight swung the hammock so low, that all the dogs on the premises were constantly rubbing their backs under me. . . ."

Another traveler at Gatun, George Schenck, witnessed an example of the natives' domestic habits which brightened his trip considerably. At breakfast Schenck and a companion named Swain were served coffee, into which they dumped the contents of the sugar bowl on the table. Schenck said, "Some other passengers came along after us, and I thought I would watch and see how they managed about their sweetening. . . . I presently saw one of the natives, a girl of about sixteen or seventeen years . . . go out and get a piece of sugar-cane, and commence chewing it, and occasionally she would eject the juice from her mouth into the coffee while it was being prepared outside the hut. Swain asked me if I was going to have some more coffee. I declined. . . ."

Taylor was roused from his hammock shortly after midnight to continue his journey upriver from Gatun, but it took two hours to get his boatmen moving. At dawn they reached the village of Dos Hermanos where they overtook two rival boats whose travelers had been successful in bribing the crews to paddle all night. Here they had breakfast. Shortly after sunrise clouds gathered threateningly. Near the rancho Palo Matilda, "a sudden cold wind came over the forests, and the air darkened. We sprang ashore and barely reached the hut, a few paces off, when the rain broke on us as if the sky had caved in. A dozen lines of white electric heat ran down, followed by crashes of thunder which I could feel throbbing in the earth under me. The rain drove into one side of the cabin and out the other, but we wrapped ourselves in India-rubber cloth and kept out the wet and chilling air."

On returning to their boat to continue their journey, they found the river rising rapidly. This forced them to hug the bank and drag themselves along by low-hanging boughs. But the river level soon fell again and they were able to continue with less frantic effort.

Taylor spent his second night on the river at Peña Blanca, where the party slept in the loft of a hut, "in the midst of the family and six other travelers." They started next morning at sunrise, hoping to reach Gorgona that night, but soon incurred a further delay by running upon a huge sunken log. The head boatman finally swam ashore with a rope in his teeth and pulled them loose.

They passed the ranchos of Agua Salud, Barro Colorado and Palenquilla before being overtaken by another storm. "We could hear the roar and the rush of the rain as it came towards us like the trampling of myriad feet on the leaves." They made fast to a sycamore and waited out that storm wrapped in their rubber ponchos.

Beyond Palenquilla, "the character of the scenery changed somewhat." The banks grew into forbidding cliffs but there were "more signs of cultivation, where the forest had been lopped away to make room for fields of maize, plantain, and rice. But many were the long and lonely reaches of the river where we glided between piled masses of bloom and greenery."

Many Yankees complained of the laziness of the boatmen, but the historian Bancroft was amazed at the strength and tenacity of his crew.

"Taking their stand upon the broadened edges of the canoe on either side, one end of their pole upon the bottom of the river, and the other placed against their shoulder, smoking with perspiration, their deep chests sending forth volumes of vapor into the vapory air, their swollen sinews strained to their utmost tension, and keeping time to a sort of grunting song, they step steadily along from stem to stern, thus sending the boat rapidly over the water, except where the current is strong. The middle of the channel, where the water is deep and the current rapid, is avoided as much as possible; yet with every precaution the men frequently miss their purchase and the boat falls back in a few minutes as great a distance as it can recover in an hour. . . ."

Each back-breaking hour the boatmen tied up their craft and plunged into the river to cool off. At intervals they would disappear into the jungle, reappearing with bottles of the fiery aguardiente from which they took frequent swigs. The passengers under the toldos did their share of drinking on the trip, passing about bottles of brandy and wine. Bursts of hilarity and snatches of song echoed along the river.

On arrival at Gorgona, a village perched high on a cliff overlooking the river, Taylor and his party decided to leave the boats and continue overland, thus disobeying a rule laid down by Joseph Gregory: "The Gorgona mule owners will advise you to take the road to Panama from that point. *Pay no attention*, for that road is totally impassable for nine months of the year. Push on without delay to Cruces. . . ." Taylor and his friends decided to avoid Cruces because cholera was reportedly prevalent there. They rented horses at Gorgona, paying ten dollars each for riding mounts and six dollars a hundredweight for baggage. After a rough trip of more than a day and a half, they arrived in Panama City.

However, most travelers at that time went on to Cruces before leaving the river, because the trail from there, as rough as it was, was better than the trail from Gorgona.

Cruces, 45 river miles from the mouth of the Chagres, had been the most important inland city of the Isthmus for two centuries, during the Spanish regime. In the old days the Gold Road from Panama City ended there. Treasure was transferred from the backs of mules to rafts and canoes and floated downriver to the sea where the Spanish galleons waited. In its golden era the vaults and warehouses of Cruces did such a volume of business that the Spanish kings leased the concession to operate them for more than 10,000 pesos a year, but when Spanish power declined, so did the importance of Cruces.

"A tolerably symmetrical arrangement of haycocks," the traveler J. Goldsborough Bruff described the place on passing through during the summer of 1851. Bruff was an intelligent, observant man, one of the best of the journal-writers. During his 24-hour stay in Cruces he saw much, and what he saw, he wrote down. In the huge, barnlike church of rough stone he observed the statues—"figures full of rags, tinsel and cobwebs." Treading across the earthen floor, hat respectfully in hand, he noted that the corners were full of trash—"wooden crosses, mutilated wooden crucifixes, broken benches, coffin-biers and more rags, more tinsel and cobwebs." The entire building was filled with the moist smell of mold and decay. Looking up he saw great holes in the ceiling and thought the roof "looked as if it might fall in at any moment."

During his first stroll around Cruces, Bruff observed through the open door of a reed hut a dead man laid out on a table. "He was dark, nearly Negro," said Bruff, "clad in a full dress-suit of black cloth with black silk stock, white standing collar and black patent leather boots." Entering the hut, his hat again respectfully in his hand, Bruff noted the jaws of the corpse were tied together to restrain the death grin with a "broad black ribbon that appeared to be silk." Candles were burning around the bier and the people kneeling on the floor kept up a continual muted groaning as though suffering physical pain. After a solemn interval Bruff tiptoed out.

He spent that night in the American Hotel in Cruces—an unpainted frame structure—paying two dollars for supper, breakfast and a cot to sleep on. During the night several of the travelers had their carpetbags rifled, but Bruff slept lying on top of his luggage and so protected his possessions from theft.

Next morning Bruff was startled to see a woman sitting up in the disarrayed bedclothes of a nearby cot, straightening her attire and combing her hair. He learned later that she was the wife of a man accused of robbery on the jungle trail. Her husband had stolen most of her possessions and deserted her. Now she spent her time wandering back and forth across the Isthmus trying to find him.

Unable to find passage until the afternoon, Bruff took another stroll and saw the funeral procession of the dead man he had seen laid out in the hut the night before. "A black-clad padre with a cross led the procession and I followed with the rest of the mourners." At the grave Bruff watched while the bier bearers chanted and rolled the body off into the open grave. With dismay Bruff saw the bearers jump into the grave "to stomp the body out straight, or," he added facetiously, "maybe to make sure he was dead." Then, while the grave was being filled, a liquor bottle was passed about from hand to hand and "the affair concluded with laughter and merriment."

Other travelers were also dismayed by the Isthmus funerals.

Daniel A. Horn, the wayfarer from Alabama, attended the funeral of a fellow Argonaut who had died of the combined effects of fever and an overdose of alcohol. "The coffin was so fragile the bottom fell out when lowered into the grave," Horn wrote home. "The grave was only two feet deep, and when the diggers showed every indication of desiring to leap into the grave and stamp the earth down on top of the coffin, they were hurled bodily away by the dead man's comrades who finished filling the grave in the respectful Christian American way." The sight made a deep impression on Horn. "Oh! How hard it seemed to die and be buried in a foreign land," he wrote.

The Cruces trail to Panama City had once been paved and some of the stonework still remained. Fragments of old Spanish paving—some huge in size—were dangerous stumbling blocks in places. The trail staggered up the steep incline to the top of the divide like the path of a drunkard and then made a rambling rush downhill. Most of the way it ran through narrow defiles which acted as drains for the torrents which fell during the wet season. The narrow gorges were muddy, rocky, sinuous, and dark from the overhang of dense tropical foliage. Moving along in single file the stumbling, slipping mules continually scraped the riders against the muddy walls. Some defiles were too narrow for two parties to pass, so before entering, the lead rider would halloo to see if anyone was already in the gorge approaching from the opposite direction.

On wider sections of the trail the way was sometimes barred by the trunks of huge fallen trees. Riding around them kept the riders continually ducking low over the necks of their mules to miss the overhanging branches of upright trees.

There were violent rain showers accompanied by flashes of lightning and tumultuous peals of thunder. The mules laid their ears back and plunged grimly forward, while the riders, with water running from them in rivulets, held to their saddle horns trying to keep their seats. Then the sun would make a sudden brief appearance, glaring down and making the jungle sizzle and steam.

Skeletons of dead mules were numerous. Vultures hunkered

in the trees patiently waiting for others to fall. Occasionally rude wooden crosses, decorated with flowers and ribbons, appeared beside the trail. These were the graves of travelers dead from fever or exhaustion. The native drovers bared their heads, crossed themselves, and sometimes had to be prevented with shoves and curses from stopping to pray before them.

With luck the travelers covered the distance from Cruces to Panama City in one day. Henry Sturdevant, who made the trip in 1851, summed it up:

"After being jolted to almost paralytic unconsciousness on the mules, alternately burned by the tropic sun and soaked by the tropic showers . . . the Argonauts hailed Panama with delight."

Panama City was two centuries old and had 8,000 to 10,000 permanent inhabitants, of whom about 2,000 could be classified as "white" by adopting a very loose definition of the term. The city, facing the sea, was backed by green mountains whose tops were generally hidden in gloomy black clouds laced with bright streaks of sun. From a distance one saw a pleasant cluster of red tile roofs surrounding the spires of several churches. The tallest were the cathedral's twin spires whose coating of pearl oyster shells glistened in the sun. On entering the city, travelers found a rat maze of alley-like streets paved with cobblestones. The two-story houses, many of wood and all painted in bright colors, had second-story verandas and balconies. Most of the streets were too narrow to allow carriages to pass and the overhanging balconies made them appear even narrower. The sidewalks, only two to three feet wide in most places, presented the same navigational problems to pedestrians. The gutters—used as sewers—were choked with filth, giving off a stench obviously most attractive to flies and roaches.

The streets were crowded with a polyglot throng. Loud-voiced Americans in red wool shirts and high boots mingled with white-suited Panamanians, Chinese in pigtails, Hindus, and citizens of all the European nations. There was a constant clatter and uproar as drays and wagons pulled by oxen, and pack trains of loaded mules, moved along the streets. From open doors sounded the clink of glasses, raucous laughter, tinny music and the slap-slap of playing cards.

"Most Americans here have thrown aside all restraint and give loose rein to evil practices," Daniel Horn wrote his mother. "I have lost all respect for American character. Here it is motivated by the twin principles of selfishness and passion."

Tropical vice did make heavy inroads on the Americans whiling away their time waiting for berths on California-bound ships. They drank themselves into delirium tremens and gambled away their grubstakes.

"Their lusts are unbridled," wrote Horn. "Good young men raised in God-fearing homes go to the dogs at a fast clip doing the clutch-and-hug dance in the arms of the painted females of the hurdy-gurdy halls."

The whores of Panama City did their best to dig their own gold in the pockets of the Argonauts, and sometimes in their shoes. "While I was engaged in pleasuring a buxom mulatress in her cubicle," wrote Joshua Sanders in his memoirs, "my feet suddenly became cool and I realized that someone had removed my shoes. Since I had secreted most of my worldly wealth—about $500 currency—in them, I immediately suspended my activities long enough to wrest the shoes from the hands of the fancy girl's macaroni who had taken them from my feet, and hurl him from the room. After putting my shoes back on and knotting the strings securely, I completed my pleasure with the wench, my Bowie knife pressed to her throat. The macaroni dared not interfere with me for fear of causing the jugular of his meal ticket to be severed. I was hot-headed in my youth and believed in getting my money's worth in all things."

All the travelers, however, did not succumb to vice; many simply hiked around town sightseeing. A favorite walk was along the East Battery fronting the bay. This battlement rose 50 feet above the beach and was 40 feet wide and 400 yards long. Lying about on the wall were long, heavy bronze cannons and piles of 32-pound shot. Some of the more erudite noted that many of the cannon bore the arms of Hispaniola and were dated "Seville

1745." From the height of this battery the Argonauts could survey the shipping in the harbor and stare longingly out to sea in search of an incoming ship.

Even when a steamer did appear, it remained maddeningly remote from the watchers on land. The harbor was so filled with silt that steamers had to stand at least two miles offshore and discharge passengers and freight into small boats for transport to the beach.

Most of the Americans, who stayed in Panama City's hotels and pensions for about eight dollars a week, slept on the plaza benches, or camped outside the city walls, were intolerant of the native citizens, and shocked by their bloody sports of cockfighting and bullbaiting. They were annoyed by the heat, the filth, the bad smells and the continual tolling of church bells. One said with grim humor that the streets were too sticky for the passage of Venetian gondolas, but entirely too liquid to walk on. "The city is dirty, noisy and unpleasant," wrote another; "if it could be Yankeeized there might be some hopes for it; but as it is, it is deplorable."

The local citizens were just as unhappy with their visitors, despite their prodigality with money. Drunken Yankees were everywhere, cursing, pushing and shoving, always in a hurry. They had no respect for the city's customs, and habitually walked through the cathedral during services, talking loudly and refusing to take off their hats.

In January 1850, a man named Judson Ames of Baton Rouge, Louisiana, arrived at Chagres on the *Falcon* with the largest and heaviest single piece of freight seen there up to that time. Fortunately for Ames, the Howland and Aspinwall steamer *Orus*, whose draft was shallow enough to allow her to cross the sand bar at the river mouth, was moored to the dock of Yankee Chagres. Summoned by the captain of the *Falcon*, the *Orus* cast loose from the wharf and chuffed out to see what was wanted. The crew of the *Falcon* rigged up a crane hoist and deposited on the deck of the *Orus* the heavy freight—a 1,200-pound Washington hand printing press, built by the R. Hoe Company of New York.

After unloading the monster on the wharf, Ames hired a flat-bottomed barge and eight natives to transport the press up the Chagres. Midstream in the river the barge suddenly tilted, and to Ames's horror, the press slid off and sank out of sight in the muddy water. "Senor Goddam" was the nickname bestowed on Ames by the native boatmen after that fiasco. Borrowing a grappling hook from the *Orus,* Ames managed to hook a line to the submerged press, organize a 20-man tug-of-war team, and pull the press almost to the bank. For half a day the native crew strained to raise the press onto the barge. Finally, in desperation, Senor Goddam jumped into the water, and according to Horace Bell, "set it on the raft without help, while the natives looked on as if he were a brother to Samson."

Lashing the press down, Ames steadied the barge by attaching a bungo boat to each side as an outrigger. After a week of strenuous paddling and poling, he reached Cruces with his printing press. There he paid $200 to hire two of the largest, strongest mules he could find. An American contractor with three matched teams of Missouri mules had just set up business in Cruces. Ames strapped mattresses to the backs of the largest pair, hitched them together side by side and laid the press across their backs. After three days of hell, Senor Goddam and his exhausted mules got their burden to Panama City.

The nearest sailing date that Ames could obtain for himself and his monster was three months away. He cleaned and oiled his press, and to occupy his time during his enforced wait, published the Panama *Herald.* One English-language newspaper was already in existence in Panama City—the *Star.* That paper had been founded the year before by several other travelers bored with waiting for a ship. The main purpose of the first edition was to chronicle their celebration of George Washington's birthday; therefore, the first issue of the *Star* was dated February 24, 1849. Afterward the *Star* appeared haphazardly every two or three weeks. When Ames finally departed from Panama City, he sold his subscription list and advertising accounts to the *Star*. The combined newspapers became the Panama *Star & Herald* and so remain to this day.

The Strip had a paper, then, but it lacked other more vital services. Law enforcement authority over Yankee Chagres and the Yankee Strip was nominally New Granada's, but the military forces of the country were so scarce and indolent that they exercised no control outside the environs of Panama City. The Panama Railroad Company had leased the town site of Yankee Chagres from New Granada as an entry port and sublet space to the other permanent residents, but the company had assumed no responsibility to govern the town and maintain order. In fact, there were no governing officials or law enforcement officers on the Yankee Strip at all. There were simply no laws. The result was anarchy. Everyone carried guns and tried to look out for his own life and property, but if he lost both, nothing official was done about it.

Increasing lawlessness greatly disturbed the express companies, charged as they were with transporting huge shipments of raw gold and specie across the 60-mile stretch of wilderness between the oceans. Like the Spanish dons before them, the companies built fortress-like treasure vaults at Chagres, Cruces and Panama City, where the gold in transit could be stored under heavy guard. When the vaults became full, the companies organized long consolidated pack trains to move the precious metal across the Isthmus.

Henry Tracy, the Wells Fargo express agent at Panama City, wrote his home office soon after his arrival on the Isthmus in 1849 darkly prophesying, "There will have to be bloodshed before matters become regulated. I have no doubt within six months there will be an attempt to seize one of the large, but half-guarded trains."

The first important robbery occurred in August 1850. Masked men attacked a Howland and Aspinwall pack train on the Cruces trail and made off into the jungle with $30,000.

Henry Tracy immediately wrote New York, "Robberies have

just commenced, and there are about a hundred as precious villains on the Isthmus as ever went unhung. . . . I am determined that there shall be none stolen from your trains without there be several funerals." To the letter Tracy attached an order for "One (1) doz. Colt revolving rifles. One (1) doz. prs. revolvers, dragoon size. One (1) doz. prs. revolvers, police size. Two (2) doz. Bowie knives. Two (2) buck shot guns. Ample powder and ball for above."

In December 1850 robbers struck a Zachrisson and Nelson mule train on the Cruces trail and took $120,000.

William A. Nelson, a partner in the express firm and also U. S. Consul at Panama City, wrote a confidential letter to William H. Aspinwall, telling him, "the so-called Derienni, the land pirates of the Isthmus as they like to call themselves, are becoming active." "Derienni" was a sinister name in Panama. Bands of home-grown highwaymen by that name in ancient times had harassed Spanish gold trains and even those of the fierce English buccaneers. Now, reinforced by the influx of hardened criminals from all over the world, they were rising again. Nelson warned Aspinwall that some drastic arrangement would have to be made "to curb these criminal excesses, or all Isthmus freight routes will be imperiled."

Several weeks later the steamship *Northerner* from San Francisco docked at Panama City with 500 successful prospectors homeward bound with their riches and a cargo of gold express in the amount of $2,600,000.

To handle this inrush the express agents in Panama City gathered all the pack animals they could find and formed a huge convoy for the trek to Chagres. Armed and mounted, the 500 miners and extra guards made a formidable array as they rode out of the city, their column stretching out almost a mile. At the Gorgona fork on the jungle trail masked horsemen attacked, yelling and firing pistols. Rearing horses whinnied and gold-laden mules broke from the line as the prospectors and express agents dropped lead ropes to grasp their weapons. A drumfire of shots echoed up and down the line.

During the melee four bandits fell mortally wounded and a few more raised their hands in surrender. But other bandits pulled several gold-laden pack mules—rearing and snorting—out of the line and transferred the gold pouches to the backs of their saddles. Mounted on fast horses, they galloped away, quickly outdistancing pursuit. When the scattered mules were gathered together again, over $100,000 in gold express was found missing.

The following months brought other robberies. Individual murders became commonplace. The killing and robbing fever began to infect even the slothful native bungo boatmen. On lonely stretches of the Chagres they knifed entire boatloads of passengers dozing under the toldos. The murderous boatmen then tossed the stripped bodies into the thick jungle on the river bank, where the ants, the land crabs and the white-shouldered vultures soon picked their bones clean. Months, sometimes a year later, a traveler was missed, but by then who could say which pile of dry bones on the jungle trail was his?

The greatest single robbery of treasure express occurred in September 1851, when the Derienni attacked a consolidated pack train near the Gorgona fork on the Cruces trail, taking $250,000 in gold and killing several express company guards. The various foreign consuls in Panama City reported this huge loss to their governments and urged the sending of foreign troops to police the Yankee Strip. When the United States and Great Britain, through diplomatic channels, requested permission of Bogotá to send such forces, the New Granadan government refused, suspecting that if foreign troops ever occupied the Isthmus, they would never be induced to leave. Bogotá sent strict orders to Governor Urrutia Aniño forbidding him to allow any armed foreign troops to land on the Isthmus.

Governor Aniño was in a quandary. His military force—all in Panama City—were the barefooted troops whose functions were to guard the military prison and enforce the collection of a two-dollar transit tax from each traveler crossing the Isthmus. Aniño saw the danger of allowing foreign troops to land, but he feared that if stern measures were not taken soon to halt the depredations of the Derienni, local governmental control would collapse. Foreign troops would then inevitably be sent and he had no means to prevent their landing, no matter how strict the orders from Bogotá were.

At this point John L. Stephens of the Panama Railroad came to the Governor with the clandestine proposal that the company be allowed to police its own right of way. Stephens assured Aniño that the large express companies favored the plan and could guarantee the cooperation of all the consular representatives. The policing would be done by *civilian* means, Stephens promised. Far removed from his seat of government and faced with grim realities close at hand, Governor Aniño reluctantly accepted the proposal as his only means of averting anarchy and foreign invasion. He signed a secret order conveying to the Panama Railroad absolute police authority over all "transients traversing the railroad right of way"—in substance, over the entire Yankee Strip. The order gave the railroad the right to punish immediately by any means whatsoever, even execution, all known highwaymen found on the right of way, without any trial or legal proceeding.

This agreement was quickly endorsed by the express companies and foreign consuls. But who would be the enforcer of the absolute power? Could a man brave enough and ruthless enough for the job be found? On being queried for suggestions, Henry Tracy, the Wells Fargo agent, answered gloomily, "I do not know of anyone you can get to come here who will not be sick part of the time. Most persons at Chagres become dissipated in a few weeks, and between drinking too much, running after women, or gambling, exhaust all their energies. When they get sick, they have no vitality left in their systems to recover. I don't know where you would find a man with the right combination of *humanity* and *inhumanity* to do the job."

The summons was sent out, but did not find its man until many more months of violence had passed.

VI

The Rival Route

TRAUTWINE AND BALDWIN, THE RAILROAD BUILDERS, HAD BROUGHT tents with them, intending to camp on Manzanillo, but the first incoming tide swamped that plan. At high tide the ocean moved in and covered the place, even the encircling rim of beach. There was not a square yard of permanently dry land on the island. All that remained visible at high tide was a dense mass of shrubbery protruding from the surface of the water. At dusk they loaded back into the bungos and returned to Chagres to seek a solution to the problem.

The forlorn hulk of an old 200-ton brigantine caught Trautwine's eye. This was one of the many reclaimed vessels used by Argonauts to get to Chagres. There she had been abandoned, as were most of the others. After beaching her the captain, crew and passengers had scrambled ashore en masse to hurry in pursuit of the golden chimera. Many other such hulks, left to rot, had been dismantled for lumber to build the shacks of Yankee Chagres. Trautwine rescued the brigantine, plugged the leaks and had the *Orus* tow her down to Manzanillo. There he anchored the derelict in the lee of the island.

Although the brigantine provided shelter, Trautwine was determined to erect a permanent structure at the Atlantic terminus. When the axemen had cleared the undergrowth from an acre or so of the island, he had them sharpen the ends of four long palm logs and drive them into the mire as pilings. On the pilings they nailed a rough plank platform and mounted a prefabricated pine shack sent down from New Orleans—the first permanent building of the future city of Colón (Aspinwall). The shack, on its high stilts, stood several feet above the water even at high tide, but the spiders, lizards and tarantulas which normally took refuge on the top branches of the shrubbery now climbed the stilts. They invaded the house in such numbers that humans could not live there, and the old brigantine remained the only livable quarters for several weeks.

Totten, returning from Cartagena on the *Orus* with a load of laborers, crowded the new arrivals onto the hulk. By now the insects and other pests had taken possession of her hold, forcing all hands up from below. The men lived and slept on deck, soaked by the rains of the approaching wet season and sickened by the constant rolling motion of the waves. During the nights retching and vomiting were frequent, making sleep almost impossible, for even with small work crews the deck of the brigantine was so crowded that the men had to sleep lying across each other's legs.

Another abandoned vessel—this one a decrepit stern-wheel steamboat named the *Telegraph*—turned up at Chagres. She had run out of coal on the voyage from New Orleans, and to feed her firebox the crew had gutted the interior, chopping up bunks and most of the deck cabin. As the *Telegraph* lay grounded on the beach, scavengers descended, stripping her of boiler, stack and paddle wheel. Determined to salvage what was left of the vessel for his own use, Trautwine boarded her with a party of construction workers, ejected the busy scavengers and towed the *Telegraph* down to Manzanillo. There, anchored alongside the brigantine, she furnished more living space for the construction workers, but relieved none of the other hardships.

John L. Stephens, President of the Panama Railroad Company, stopped at Manzanillo en route from Bogotá to the United States. After looking over the situation, he sent Totten to Cartagena for additional men and took Trautwine to New York with him to report to the directors on the progress of construction. Work continued on Manzanillo with a crew directed by James Baldwin. The rainy season was at its height. The men sloshed about in the water, swinging axes and machetes at the undergrowth while the rains drifted down on them in steaming clouds. In the brief periods of sunlight which occasionally interrupted the rains, the vegetation crackled with a magical growth that threatened to cover cleared areas faster than the crews could beat it down. At night Baldwin and his men dragged back to the hulks, there to pitch and toss in uneasy sleep, soaked by the rain and ravaged by insects.

Late in July John Trautwine returned from the States with half a dozen new assistant engineers. He brought also David F. Rogers, a road contractor from New Orleans, and a group of fifty Irish laborers. Rogers had won a contract from the Panama Railroad Company to build a plank road from Navy Bay to Panama City to carry Isthmian traffic while the railroad was under construction. The plan was short-lived, however, as were most of the laborers. The Irishmen died so rapidly from fever that only two miles of road were completed before the survivors decided to escape with their lives. Totten and Trautwine were amazed at the speed with which the oak planking on the road decayed. Within a few months the heavy wood had crumbled into dirt and no trace of it remained.

Despite the hardships and the casualties, work progressed. By August 1 they had cleared Manzanillo of undergrowth. This reduced the number of insects and forced the alligators and other reptiles to retreat to the mainland. By the end of the month they had exterminated enough of the insects to allow men to live in the stilted shack. The labor force swelled to 400 and other shacks on stilts arose around the original one.

Although the mosquitoes were fewer, they had done a deadly

work. Men dropped in gasping prostration from the fever planted in their blood. Working waist-deep in water, many fell over and simply disappeared, a few brief bubbles marking their passage. No one was spared. Totten, Trautwine, Baldwin and their assistants each alternated between a week of work and a week of sweating delirium. They had no doctors and no medicines; in fact, they did not know what brought the fever. There were several theories about its cause: "pestilential vapors," "ardent sun," "northerly winds" and "highly electrical conditions of the atmosphere." The death rate on the railroad work crew grew to one in five every month. The fear of death caused the workers to desert in great numbers. The paymaster began holding back the men's pay to keep them on the job, but still they ran off.

Dr. J. A. Totten, brother of George M. Totten, came down to build the first railroad hospital on the Isthmus—another grass-roofed, stilted shack on Manzanillo. The mortality rate among his patients was so high that disposition of their dead bodies became a problem. At first they were buried at sea and the surviving kindred, if known, were notified by letter. In many cases, however, the names of relatives were not known because the man himself was almost anonymous, carried on work rolls by only a first name or a nickname. With these anonymous bodies Dr. Totten began a practice that continued throughout the entire five years of railroad construction: he pickled them in large barrels, kept them for a decent interval to be claimed, and then sold them in wholesale lots to medical schools all over the world. Then, as now, human cadavers available for scientific purposes were in short supply. The bodies brought high prices, and the profit from the sale of the cadavers made the railroad hospital self-sustaining during the construction years.

The four-mile perimeter of Manzanillo, built up above sea level before the island center was filled in, soon displayed a line of grass-roofed shacks standing like a row of dejected herons on the banks of a pond. The central lagoon shrank gradually as fill was dumped in. The railroad company leased the newly created dry land to private businessmen who opened saloons, stores and gambling halls. Docks went up around the island to serve the ships which arrived daily bringing construction material, machinery and humanity of many varieties. The first females classifiable as permanent residents were 50 prostitutes from Cartagena. They were soon joined by others from Havana and New Orleans. Nights sounded with the whining scrape of fiddles and drunken laughter.

By the end of August the 400-man work force had cut a swath two miles through the swamp to the first high ground—a wooded ridge called Monkey Hill after the simian multitudes swinging in the trees there. Later, when it became the site of the first cemetery of the Panama Railroad, Monkey Hill was renamed Mount Hope. After leaving this ridge, the railroad line, as projected, would cross four more miles of swamp and then two miles of solid ground before reaching the bank of the Chagres opposite Gatun.

Totten put Baldwin in charge of construction on Manzanillo Island and sent another crew up the Chagres to Gatun to begin construction from there back toward the sea. Two small river steamers, the *Aspinwall* and the *Gorgona,* began daily trips from Yankee Chagres to Gatun, dumping supplies and additional men.

Baldwin, faced with grading the right of way in the swamp, had the worst assignment. To eliminate a daily trip back and forth, his crew carried rude planks on their backs to Monkey Hill and built a shack on the cut-off stumps of trees to raise it above water level. He and his crew worked waist-deep in slimy water, surrounded by alligators and snakes. The alligators sometimes attacked workers who strayed too far from the group, so many of the men carried revolvers as well as machetes to fight off the swimming reptiles. The white men wore huge cork helmets, called "elephant hats," on their heads and long gauze veils to cover their faces, but the bareheaded natives worked in short cotton pants, stolidly ignoring the flies and mosquitoes. At night, returning to their clammy shack, they all slept with exhaustion despite the howls of jaguars and other startling night sounds from the surrounding jungle.

With the advent of the dry season in December of 1850, the work force rose occasionally to almost 1,000 men, but labor attrition was so heavy that every two weeks or so Totten had to send a steamer to Cartagena for more. Desertions, disease and the lure of the gold fields took many of the workers, but there was now another manpower thief on the Isthmus.

After being paid on Saturdays, the whole crew departed from the miserable island for the fleshpots of Yankee Chagres. They found there, in addition to the usual deterrents to returning to Manzanillo, the seductive agents of Commodore Cornelius Vanderbilt, offering higher wages to lure them away. A Vanderbilt steamer stood just offshore, whistle tooting in short, urgent blasts, anxious to carry off as many as would go.

The overpowering smell of money had brought the predatory Vanderbilt to Central America to compete with the Panama Railroad for the revenues of the California passage. The Commodore had developed a project of his own to provide a continental crossing for California-bound travelers and he needed all the workers he could steal from the Panama Railroad. His raids were so devastating that Totten had to double his laborer's wage from 40 cents to 80 cents a day to compete with him.

Corporate profits were behind it. During 1849 and 1850 George Law's United States Mail Steam Line ships, with their crowded, foul-smelling staterooms and steerages, grossed over $3,000,000 on the New York to Chagres run. Commodore Vanderbilt, shipowner, master of the New York ferry system, and bitter rival of George Law, decided to get into the Panama game. Thereafter he made several unsuccessful attempts to break Law's government franchise and bully his way into the management of the United States Mail Steam Line and the Panama Railroad Company.

While smarting from repeated rebuffs, Vanderbilt read the numerous newspaper reports recounting tribulations of passengers traveling the Panama Route—the wails of multitudes who waited in Panama City for ships that never came while their capital melted and many died. These newspaper reports, widely circulated in the East, caused many prospective California travelers to shun the Panama Route. Vanderbilt decided to exploit this anti-Panama publicity by promoting a new route across the land barrier. In addition to making large profits, Vanderbilt could realize his dream of crushing Law and Aspinwall, or at least of bringing them to heel.

In early 1849 the Commodore's family noticed that he spent much of his time at home perusing large colored maps which he kept secreted in a locked desk drawer. Most of these maps were of Nicaragua, 300 miles north of Panama where the tapering land mass of Central America narrowed to a width of 165 miles. From San Juan del Norte on the Caribbean coast, Commodore Vanderbilt's finger traced the twisting, turning line of the San Juan River upstream 120 miles to the river's point of origin, the southeast corner of Lake Nicaragua. Lake Nicaragua, more than 100 miles long, the largest lake in Central America, had once been a bay in the Pacific Coast. The outer edge had been sealed off from the ocean by volcanic upheaval in prehistoric times and the waters had gradually become fresh from the influx of mountain streams. The salt-water life in the sealed-off bay had adapted to the new environment. Such ocean types as sharks and tarpon abounded in the lake. The volcanic ridge separating the lake from the Pacific Ocean was only 12 miles wide at its narrowest and there were supposed to be notches in this ridge which might be deepened to reinstitute the water connection between lake and sea.

The Nicaragua crossing had been known to the Spaniards for more than 300 years. They had used it in the old days when British freebooters were lurking offshore at Panama City or Porto Bello. The land barrier was almost three times as wide as at Panama, but crossing there shortened the sea distance from New York to San Francisco by almost 500 nautical miles. Also, except for the narrow ridge on the Pacific side, Nicaragua theoretically offered an all-water route, and an all-water route was what Vanderbilt was after, because it might be converted into a canal. No railroad could compete with a canal in number of passengers and volume of freight. Building a canal across Nicaragua would be the most dramatic way to capture all trans-Isthmian business, confound his rivals and render their projected strip of tracks across Panama worthless. With a Nicaragua canal in operation the steamships of Law and Aspinwall would have to abandon Panama or go bankrupt. The Panama Railroad Company would be crushed. The Commodore could then impose what tolls he wished on his competitors' ships and pile up tremendous profits for years to come.

Successful crossings at Nicaragua had been made early in the Gold Rush. In February 1849 George Gordon of Philadelphia organized "Gordon's California Association," chartered the *Mary*, a small brig, and advertised: "a $260 first-class passage from New York to San Juan de Nicaragua, from thence per Steam Boat *Plutus* to Granada, on Lake Managua; or, navigation permitting, to Managua, Matiares or Nagarote on Lake Leon, as may be convenient for landing; and a passage from Realejo, on the Pacific, to San Francisco with Hammock, Bed, and Bedding for the voyage and camp accommodations during detention on land, en route." Gordon said he had an agent on the Pacific to charter ships at Panama City and Acapulco and send them to Realejo, Nicaragua, to pick up the group. Any fear that no idle ship might be found on the Pacific Coast was supposed to be dispelled by the final paragraph of the advertisement: "In the unexpected event of vessels not being procured, $75 of the passage money and 60 days' provisions will be refunded each passenger at Realejo, which will procure passage on the mail steamers which will pass there." The phrase "pass there" was apt. Realejo was not a scheduled stop for the Pacific Mail Steamship Company which operated the mail steamers, and these crowded vessels would certainly "pass" Realejo by. Just how this reimbursement of money and provisions would induce the steamers to put in for an unscheduled stop was not set forth in the advertisement.

Enthusiasm for a quick passage to California was so high that a capacity load of 136 passengers—many of them recent Yale graduates—bought tickets from Gordon and sailed on the *Mary*. At San Juan del Norte the Gordon party disembarked and waited while the little steamer *Plutus,* shipped on the *Mary* disassembled, was put together. The party drank or gambled during the day and during the evenings the Yale crowd entertained them with college songs and theatrical skits. Three weeks later, after several futile attempts by the *Plutus* to ascend the river, the party was still there. So they had to hire bungos, just as their counterparts were doing in Panama, to go on. The trip upriver and across the lake to Granada took them until the middle of April. No arrangements had been made at Granada for mules, and pack animals were in short supply because buyers from the Panama Route had stripped the area. The party finally obtained enough mounts to shuttle them to Realejo a few at a time. They sailed July 20 from Realejo on a small brigantine, the *Laura Ann,* and after a long, uncomfortable voyage landed in San Francisco in early October, more than eight months after leaving New York.

Not discouraged by the saga of the Gordon party, Vanderbilt sent an agent, Colonel David L. White, to Nicaragua to obtain a concession. White, with the help of E. G. Squier, the United States *charge d'affaires,* managed to negotiate a contract for a canal with the Nicaraguan government in which Vanderbilt agreed to pay Nicaragua $10,000 at once, then $200,000 in company stock, and $10,000 a year until construction was completed. The canal had to be built within twelve years and then the company would pay Nicaragua 20 per cent of the net profits for 85 years. At the end of that period the canal would become the property of Nicaragua. In the contract Vanderbilt also provided for his company to have exclusive rights over any railroad, carriage road, or river transportation utilized during the period while the canal was being dug. He formed the American Atlantic and Pacific Ship Canal Company to work out plans for the canal project, and the Accessory Transit Company which would begin carrying travelers and baggage across Nicaragua at once by any means which he could devise.

Vanderbilt purchased the steamer *Orus,* then on duty as a tender in the harbor of Chagres, and sent her to Nicaragua bearing Colonel Orville W. Childs, a military engineer, to survey the routes for both the canal and the interim transportation. Colonel Childs was not afflicted with the ebullient optimism of his counterpart on the Isthmus, Colonel G. W. Hughes. Childs's opinion of the San Juan River was that the lower half, nearest the Caribbean coast, was unnavigable, being much too shallow in the dry season. The upper half of the river, between the Castillo Falls and Lake Nicaragua, he judged navigable the year around. In the volcanic ridge separating the lake and the ocean he found a depression only 46 feet above the surface of the lake and 153 feet above mean sea level. This, the lowest gap in the Continental Divide between the Arctic Circle and the Straits of Magellan, was 120 feet lower than the lowest elevation found on the Panama Route.

Childs estimated that a Nicaragua canal would take six years to build and cost over $31,000,000. His conception was a canal 17 feet deep and 50 feet wide at the bottom with a waterline breadth of 78 feet in rock and 118 feet in soft earth. Childs's locks were to be 250 feet long by 60 feet wide. The Childs concept obviously called for the construction of special boats for the canal since the waterway as described would not accommodate even the small ocean-going steamers of the 1850's.

When Vanderbilt's agreement with Nicaragua became known, international objections arose. Great Britain also had dreams of a Nicaragua canal. Her adventures there had begun years earlier. In 1780, to punish Spain for supporting the American Revolution, the British sent Horatio Nelson, then a 21-year-old captain in the Royal Navy, to lead a 200-man force to sack and burn Castillo Viejo, the principal Spanish fort. Nelson took his force ashore at San Juan del Norte and then up the San Juan River to the lake. He did destroy the fort and set the garrison to flight, but it was a Pyrrhic victory. All but ten of his 200 men died of a malignant fever contracted on the march. Nelson himself, stricken with the fever, barely survived and remained a semi-invalid for the rest of his life as a result.

After the exodus of the Spanish from Nicaragua, Great Britain established a protectorate on the Caribbean side of the country over a strip of territory called the Mosquito Coast. In 1848 the Mosquito Coast revolted and declared its independence from Nicaragua. The British built a customhouse at San Juan del Norte, the principal port controlling the entrance to the vital San Juan River, and anglicized the transaction by renaming the port "Greytown."

Controlling the only feasible Caribbean terminus for a Nicaragua canal, the British could block any project they desired. And it became obvious that the British wanted no part of a canal scheme engineered by the Yankee pirate Cornelius Vanderbilt.

Secretary of State John M. Clayton and the British Minister, Sir Henry Lytton Bulwer, after long conferences, finally agreed that if the United States would relinquish exclusive control of any Nicaragua canal and share it with Great Britain, then the British would withdraw their objections and even make capital available to help pay construction costs. Vanderbilt, won over by the prospect of British funds, relaxed his firm stand on exclusive U. S. control. The Clayton-Bulwer Treaty was signed and Vanderbilt set off for England to make financial arrangements with the British bankers.

Vanderbilt had been outfoxed. The British bankers refused to underwrite canal construction in Nicaragua. The cost was too high, they said. They had not committed themselves as parties to the diplomatic treaty and could not be coerced into risking their money on a Yankee project. So, the United States was saddled with a treaty binding it to joint control with the British over any Nicaragua canal, no matter who built it or paid the cost.

While Vanderbilt was fighting his frustrating battle with the British bankers and his engineer Colonel Childs was making gloomy predictions about the cost of a Nicaragua canal, more people were actually crossing there.

H. D. Pierce of New York City, who had been in California since August 1849, landed at Realejo on the west coast of Nicaragua in the middle of November 1850, homeward bound. Pierce traveled to Leon by cart, stopping overnight at villages on the way, paying six dollars for the privilege of "being carried with my baggage when I chose to ride."

"The country is beautiful but a perfect wilderness," said Pierce, ". . . inhabited by Monkeys Birds & Serpants & beasts of prey."

He surveyed Leon, capital of Nicaragua, "a large and ancient town containing 40,000 inhabitants . . ." and noted its few wonders, mostly ecclesiastical:

"The Cathedral is an imence building being 350 feet long & 170 wide. The roof is built on Many arches & the whole structure is brick & stone Morter & Sement. It was 18 years in building & cost $1,800,000. The view from the church is verry extensive. There are 13 churches. There are many ruins in & about the Citty. No commercial or Mecanical opperations are carried on, except Shoe Makers & some small traders . . . The Natives are verry friendly & think much of the Americans . . ."

The next portion of Pierce's route, skirting the shore of Lake Managua, was scenically beautiful, but the road was the faintest trace—"not an hours work had been done on it . . . only to cut the Brush out of the way. It crooks & dodges about to Shun trees & mudholes."

The voyage in native boats along the shore of Lake Nicaragua from Granada to San Carlos, the village at the origin of the San Juan River, took six days. Pierce's group camped on the bank at night and crept along the shore during the days, alternately drenched by rain and scorched by sun. The 120-mile descent of the swift-moving San Juan to the Caribbean took only two days, but such speed was of little consequence, since there was no ship waiting in the harbor of San Juan del Norte when they arrived. It was now December 7—Pierce's passage across Nicaragua from west to east had taken three weeks.

Even as the Argonauts on the Panama Route, Pierce and his companions had to resign themselves to a long period of waiting for a ship in an unfriendly foreign port. San Juan del Norte had even less to recommend it than Panama City.

"The inhabitants are composed of Germans French English & Musketoes or natives which predominates. The Americans have well nigh eat them out of house & home . . . as they raise nothing about here. Went to board with an old German Lady at $1.25 per day. From the lake to this place there is not a house nor any improovement of any kind except such as is made by the Alligators. . . ."

As they waited, other groups straggled in from the west until the miserable rain-soaked town was ready to burst its seams with unwelcome visitors. The British consul, alarmed at the number of unrestrained Yankees overflowing the British protectorate, impressed a man-of-war then in the harbor—the frigate *Inflexible*—to take Pierce and 500 of his companions to Chagres. Just outside the harbor, the *Inflexible* met a Chagres-bound steamer and transferred the passengers. "We paid an ounce (of gold) each for about 30 hours run," said Pierce.

Arriving at Chagres, Pierce managed to obtain passage on the *Crescent City* to New York. He landed there January 8, 1851, three months after leaving San Francisco.

Meanwhile, Colonel Orville W. Childs, Vanderbilt's engineer in Nicaragua, wrecked the *Orus* in the San Juan River trying to ascend the rushing waters to Lake Nicaragua. The colonel sent his employer a letter saying that because of the rapids and the submerged rocks, steamer transportation was not possible on the San Juan River. "Not possible" was not in Vanderbilt's vocabulary. Reading the message on his return to New York, Vanderbilt refused to accept his engineer's opinion. He had companies formed, contracts signed, and stock ready to be sold. He went down to Nicaragua at once in his new 1,500-ton side-wheeler *Prometheus,* towing behind a small, shallow-draft steamer, the *Director*. On arrival at San Juan del Norte, Vanderbilt took the helm of the *Director* personally. After tying down the safety valve, he "put on all steam and charged upriver, jumping all obstacles," forcing the little *Director* to scrape and struggle over all shoals and submerged rocks.

At the Castillo rapids he met an eight-foot waterfall, too high to be "jumped." Here the old mariner showed his onlookers how to warp the little steamer up over the falls by using capstans and ropes tied to trees. On New Year's Day 1850 he steered the *Director* into Lake Nicaragua, having personally piloted her the entire 120-mile trip upriver.

After exploring the western shore of the lake, Vanderbilt decided to make his crossing of the ridge through a notch opposite Virgin Bay. Then he began raiding the Panama Railroad for laborers to build a 12-mile planked road. On the Pacific side he built a brand new town to serve as a port, naming it San Juan del Sur. To bring passengers from New York to the Caribbean side of Nicaragua, Vanderbilt intended to use his new steamer *Prometheus*. He sent another new steamer, the 1,100-ton *Pacific*, around Cape Horn to serve on the run from San Juan del Sur to San Francisco. For the lake and the upper reaches of the San Juan River he used the *Director* and another steamer, *Central America*. The waterfall at Castillo continued to be a stumbling block so he made a portage there. Two small iron-hulled steamers, *The John M. Clayton* and *The Sir Henry Bulwer*, were put on the river below the Castillo falls. Many of the rocks were blasted out, but the river remained so shallow that the metal hulls of the little ships emitted loud groans and screeches as they scraped upstream. On reaching the falls, passengers disembarked and climbed over the ridge on foot to board one of the larger steamers for the trip to the lake and across.

Service across Nicaragua, called the Transit Route during that era, began in the summer of 1851. On July 4, 1851, Vanderbilt's first shipload of passengers arrived in San Francisco on the *Pacific*.

An editorial in the New York *Herald*, the oracle of all matters pertaining to the Gold Rush, said glowingly:

"Captain Vanderbilt and his associates on the Nicaragua Route and George Law and his associates on the Panama Route will hasten the state of things destined soon to occur, when the government and institutions of the United States will be extended over the whole of Mexico and Central America."

Pairing the two archenemies in such a blithe manner was like trying to mate a dog and cat. The two were not out to hasten any manifest destiny of the United States in Mexico and Central America, nor were they trying to improve the lot of mankind. They were out to eat each other alive. And thus the war of the Central American routes began.

Working long hours to clear and resurface their soggy island, Totten and Trautwine were harassed by Commodore Vanderbilt's raids on their labor force, but knew little of his progress in Nicaragua. Arriving ships brought reports of the activities in the harbor at San Juan del Norte, but what was going on inland was a matter of conjecture. Some said Vanderbilt was digging a canal, some said he was building a road, and others said that revolutions in the country were on the verge of driving him out completely. It was all rumor and hearsay to the toilers on the island.

After Manzanillo was cleared and filled in with enough solid earth to furnish a base on which to work, the contractors began building a causeway across the channel to the mainland on which to lay the railroad tracks. In December 1850 the company sent down pile-driving equipment by steamer from New York. The pile driver was mounted on a floating platform in the channel. A black iron steam engine, wheezing like a giant tea kettle, slowly raised a heavy mass of iron to the top of a derrick-like frame. The weight hesitated for a second at the top and then whizzed down to land on the butt of a pitch-soaked log with a loud *chunk*. The steady *chunk-chunk-chunk* of the pile driver went on all day, beating the timbers into the soggy channel bottom. This original causeway of timber piling and crib work was later replaced by a solid wall of stone and earth. Over the years the wall was widened until the entire channel was filled in, so that Manzanillo became permanently part of the mainland, and the site of the present city of Colón.

The channel bottom proved more solid than the marshy shore line of the mainland. With the help of the pile driver they soon put the causeway across the channel, but the gelatinous terrain of the mainland swallowed huge amounts of ballasting fill without apparent effect. For weeks forward progress was at a standstill while a constantly moving chain of mule-drawn carts inched across the causeway, dumping crushed rock into the seemingly bottomless mire. When Baldwin made his first sounding, he found solid earth at 180 feet. After dumping 3,000 tons of rock, the sounding still showed 180 feet. Baldwin theorized that the fill was simply spreading out below the surface and disappearing.

Totten made a wide search for a supply of stone fill. At Bohío on the Chagres he found an abandoned sandstone quarry. The rock was soft, but sound and quarryable. River steamers pulled lighters full of the broken stone downriver to the sea and along the coast to Manzanillo for dumping into the swamp. The quarry was more valuable to the Panama Railroad than a gold mine. Without that supply of fill the roadbed would never have left the edge of Manzanillo Channel.

In February 1851 the first rolling stock came ashore: a steam locomotive built by M. W. Morris & Co. of Philadelphia and a string of gondola cars. They laid rails from the wharf across the island and the locomotive began shuttling gondolas loaded with crushed rock to the end of the track, building up the causeway. The native laborers, on seeing for the first time the locomotive puffing smoke and fire like a dragon and hearing the piercing shriek of the whistle, ran off the job and into the jungle. They finally became used to the engine's smoky noise, but generally kept their distance from it.

When track was laid on the causeway, Totten sent the locomotive pushing more cars of crushed rock into the swamp, feeding the muck of the mainland. With the help of the locomotive the tracks reached Monkey Hill, two miles from the terminus, in another month. Totten established the official railroad cemetery at Monkey Hill, and during construction, a funeral train ran daily from Manzanillo to the cemetery.

The next locomotive came equipped with a dump instead of a cowcatcher and was put to building up the surface of Manzanillo itself. The interior lagoon soon disappeared as a permanent body of water. However, for years during the rainy season the interior of the island was a sopping marsh, crisscrossed with raised wooden sidewalks.

Beyond Monkey Hill the rails followed the southern and eastern shores of Navy Bay for three miles, until they struck the Mindi River about 1,000 yards upstream from the river's mouth. This was a three-mile stretch of quicksand and bottomless sink-holes. Totten chained flatcars together and sank them in sections to make a floating, hammock-like base for the roadbed. Once rails were laid, the trains carried loads of rock to be dumped on each side of the right of way. Totten prayed that the fill would hold the floating foundation steady. This practice was, in general, successful. However, at times during the years to come, entire strings of flatcars left standing too long in one spot on this section of track would disappear. Track walkers would find only a muddy blank on the right of way—cars and trackage had sunk out of sight.

The Mindi, a narrow, sluggish stream whispering along the bottom of a deep ravine almost hidden under the overhang of tropical foliage, made a bend that barred the way. They had to cut through acres of tough bamboo to clear enough area near the stream for building a bridge. The river abounded in alligators, many of great size. The white men, urged on by the natives, shot them in great number for sport. The natives, valuing alligator oil for medication and alligator teeth for charms, triumphantly pulled the dead reptiles ashore and hacked them up with machetes.

The Mindi bridge was built of wood, the first of many wooden bridges. However, decay was so malignant that these bridges had to be rebuilt every six to eight months. Ultimately most were replaced with iron.

While the bridge building went on, Baldwin made notes describing his surroundings. He noted that the trees were palm, cedar and espabe, giants towering 100 feet in the air. He was amazed at the fantastic variety of parasitic growths. Many of these, after completely covering a tree, took on the victim's outward appearance to a remarkable degree. Only by close scrutiny could it be seen that what looked like a tree was in reality a hollow shell supporting the parasite alone; the tree had disappeared in the process. Baldwin theorized that one variety of parasite sprang from seeds deposited in the ordure of birds in the highest branches of the trees. These sent long fibrous tendrils cascading to earth, where they took root. Once rooted, the tendrils sometimes grew to six inches in diameter. Ultimately the tree became so decayed and depleted from succoring its deadly companion that it would have fallen had not the parasite held it erect. "A tree in that condition is like a soul destroyed by sin," said the religious Baldwin. "The process goes on in a deadly inevitable way until the tree is irrevocably entwined."

Baldwin was not a botanist, but he had a lively interest in his surroundings and an eye for detail. The numerous varieties of palms interested him, especially those used by the natives in their daily lives. The oil palm trees were greater in size than the tasseled palms, he noted. Instead of gaudy tassels, the oil palms bore large clusters of scarlet nuts, the size of limes, hanging from the topmost foliage by single stems two or three feet in length. Baldwin described the "wine" palm whose sap was fermented, the sago palm which furnished starch, the "ivory" palm which bore the vegetable ivory nuts, the "glove" palm which gave the natives spathe—sac-like sheathing for ready-made bags capable of holding as much as half a bushel of grain—and the "cabbage" palm whose tender shoots on the treetops resembled that vegetable in appearance and taste. Baldwin mentioned still other types of palm trees from which the natives made flax, sugar, utensils and weapons.

After crossing the Mindi River bridge, the roadbed ran for two miles over firmer terrain to reach the Chagres opposite Gatun. Here the river was about 50 yards wide, making a great bend which opened beautiful vistas through the forest of giant trees. Standing on the eastern bank, a hilly ridge, Baldwin could see across the river a broad savanna which extended back a mile or more to a range of dark green hills. At the foot of these hills were the huts of Gatun.

The rails reached the river opposite Gatun in April 1851. According to railroad legend, this event was celebrated only by an Irish construction foreman and his gang who got drunk on native rum and fired off a rusty old arquebus left over from the pirate days.

The tracks were only a mile from Gatun, but the rainy season had begun and that last mile was described in the Panama *Herald* as "one of the worst and most ugly pestiferous marshes on the Continent." Fever struck the engineering staff during the critical planning stages of the attack on the swamp. Again work almost stopped.

In order to salvage something from the period, Totten sent J. C. Campbell, a civil engineer who had escaped the fever, inland with a crew to survey the route beyond Gatun. At Barbacoas Campbell found the way again barred by the Chagres, flowing through a deep canyon. A large, complicated bridge would have to be built here, Campbell notified Totten. Then he continued his survey on toward Panama City.

The trackage across the swamp to Gatun was at last completed during the first week of September. The first work train traveled the distance from Manzanillo to Gatun on October 1, 1851, eight miles of railroad which had taken 20 months to build and cost over $1,000,000.

The news from New York was bad, very bad. The company was out of money. The directors called for another stock subscription, but Wall Street had heard of the terrible difficulties delaying construction and of the mushrooming graveyard on Monkey Hill. Vanderbilt's agents were diligent in spreading tales of the bottomless swamps and deadly fevers of the Isthmus. The Commodore's Transit Route across Nicaragua was now in full swing, with two steamers on the lower San Juan River, two steamers on Lake Nicaragua, and carriages on the 12-mile planked road across the ridge to the Pacific. Although Vanderbilt's steamers were commonly referred to in the press as "floating pigsties," and on several occasions an effigy in a coffin was displayed on the San Francisco streets—an effigy placarded "Vanderbilt's Death Line"—his route, when all connections were made properly, was several days faster than the Panama Route. And Vanderbilt was a rate-cutter. His lower fares alone were enough to drain many passengers from Panama had there been no saving in time at all.

Panama Railroad stock took a bearish nosedive. The new issue went begging and the outstanding stock began to be peddled in the bucket shops for ten cents a share and finding few takers.

William H. Aspinwall and John L. Stephens tried to keep the project going on their own personal credit, but the undertaking was too expensive. The flow of materials diminished to a trickle and then dried up. The work force was reduced to a few engaged only in maintenance, trying to protect the completed roadbed from the forces of climate and spreading jungle. John Trautwine, bored with the inactivity, turned in his resignation to accept an engineering commission in Philadelphia. He shook hands all around and sailed for the States. By late November 1851, with the tracks reaching to Miller's Station three miles beyond Gatun, the Panama Railroad Company seemed on the edge of bankruptcy.

VII

The Hangman

IN THE FALL OF 1850 A STRANGER RODE OUT ON A MULE FROM SAN Antonio, Texas, to have words with Randolph Runnels, the famous Ranger and Indian killer abiding under his own vine and fig tree on the Colorado River. The man was guided by a young Mexican boy riding a burro, "scarcely larger than a large dog," Runnels' sister Octavia recalled. "We children gawked at the stranger because he wore black store clothes and a stiff black stovepipe hat. We had never seen anyone like him before. Our mother made us go up the ladder to the cabin loft, but she remained below and stared through the chinking at the man as he sat on the gallery talking with Randolph."

The stranger was an official of the Howland and Aspinwall Company. He sat in a cane-bottomed chair, sipped a cup of mustang grape wine, and told Runnels the purpose of his visit. Colonel Jack Hays, Sheriff of San Francisco, had sent him, the stranger said. According to Hays, Runnels was highly qualified for a mission of great importance on the Isthmus of Panama.

Because the man had been sent by Jack Hays, a lifelong friend,

Runnels allowed the stranger to speak his piece, even though the talk brought back unpleasant memories of a time of darkness and blood when he had pursued violence for the sinful excitement of the senses.

"The place of passage across the Isthmus—called the Yankee Strip—is ten miles wide and 40 miles from sea to sea as the crow flies," said the stranger. "I have not seen it myself, but I have it on good authority that it's the most terrible wilderness on the face of the earth, sir. To cross from Chagres on the Atlantic side to Panama City on the Pacific, you must travel several days by native canoe upriver. . . . The river is full of snakes and crocodiles, I understand. The fever is hellish, sir. When it strikes, you may not wake in the morning. We are trying to transport gold express by pack train and are attempting to build a railroad. We are sorely harassed by the fiercest group of cutthroats and highwaymen ever to walk the earth. We need a man there who has the courage and ability to deal with them."

Randolph Runnels nodded. It was as his preacher Jesse Hord had prophesied: a great river full of demons and monsters and a pestilence that walked by darkness. The stranger in the black store suit and hard hat was the searching wind sent by the Lord to seek him out. "I have been waiting for two years," said Randolph Runnels. "I am ready to go."

"I take up my pen to write this down in an earnest effort to leave behind a small chip or leaf on the Shores of Time 'ere the small river of my life wends its way to the sea and is forever lost in the Bounding Main." These are the words of Octavia Charity Marsden, nee Runnels, written in her old age while living her last years as a resident of the Confederate Home in Austin, where, as the surviving widow of a sergeant major of Hood's Texas Brigade, she had every right to be. The "small chip or leaf" left behind is a thin bundle of pages covered with handwriting in ink that has turned brown with time. The penmanship is angular and sometimes staggers into incomprehensible snarls. In places religious exhortations break in. "The Kingdom is nigh!" she will say, or, "Yea, I know my Redeemer liveth!" These happen when an irresistible manifestation of the Almighty Presence comes suddenly upon her. But mostly the thoughts of Mrs. Marsden are clear, lucid and unbroken, and her script is as delicate and strong as strands of fine brown wire.

"My brother Randolph from his early youth," she wrote, "though a fond and loving brother, was skilled in the tricks and arts of sin and the modes of predatory warfare." This was written in 1930. Octavia Marsden, living out of one time and into another, had found the peace of God. Gone was the bitterness of being left a childless widow at 19 and forsaken by her only brother, who had not chosen to return from the wilderness of Central America to stand with the righteous and contribute his considerable talent for warfare to the Lost Cause.

"I must set down first the manner of my brother's appearance," wrote Mrs. Marsden. "He was slight of stature and sensitive to any mention of the subject. None the less he was handsome, with a fair complexion, brown eyes and brown silky hair. He was graceful of his walk and vain of his hands, which were as swift and sure as hummingbirds. My first memory of him is as a youth returning from campaigning against the bloody Comanche with Colonel Hays."

Mrs. Marsden, having been born about 1839, was a small child during the 1840's when the group of Rangers under Colonel Jack Hays fought the Comanches at Plum Creek and Uvalde Canyon, using the huge five-shot Walker Colts against the red men for the first time. The weapons effected many casualties as the Rangers stood firm and fired methodically into the dusty swarm of yelling attackers. Later Randolph Runnels went with Colonel Hays to the Mexican War, serving at Vera Cruz as a pack train leader. He was one of the riders clad in their underwear who swam the bare-backed horses in from the transports and brought them, grunting in protest, splashing through the surf to Collado beach to follow Worth's Brigade inland for the siege of the city.

"Although my brother was considered a Godless man in his youth," said Mrs. Marsden, "there came a time when he changed, the occasion of which I shall describe. We were visiting our relatives at Big Caney Bayou in East Texas. The Reverend Jesse Hord, a famous preacher, gave a sermon one night and it was as though Randolph were touched with a tongue of fire. He made a clear, pentecostal conversion. No matter what violent acts he performed later, I know that he did them in the sure knowledge that he was saved and washed in the blood of the Lamb."

Reverend Hord, with the flames of a huge log fire casting fearful shadows and flickerings across the faces of his listeners, preached of hell and the eternal burning torment awaiting sinners there. At the end of the sermon when he dropped to his knees, arms outstretched, and begged the sinners to flee the Lord's wrath by professing Christ as the Son of God, many of the onlookers were so moved they fell to the ground and cried aloud for mercy. Several, twitching as though stricken with the St. Vitus Dance, began mouthing the Unknown Tongue.

Randolph Runnels did not fall to the ground, cry aloud or weep, but it was evident that he had undergone a significant spiritual experience. Later, in the privacy of a family gathering in a cabin, Reverend Hord summed it up, "Brother Runnels, I know you have spent your life in folly and the haunts of wickedness—horse-swapping, gambling, racing and the pursuit of painted women."

Here, even in the religious convictions of great age, Mrs. Marsden allowed a sisterly loyalty to creep through. "Sometimes I feel that those men chosen to spread the Lord's word are prone to imagine too much vice in their fellow men. If my brother Randolph ever experienced a carnal thought, he never expressed it to my memory. In the presence of ladies he was always a courteous gentleman."

Reverend Hord went on to say that he knew that Runnels had shed blood, not only that of the painted savage but also that of white Christian men.

In regard to that statement, Mrs. Marsden recalled, "I know of two white men, strangers and rough-looking, who had the temerity to steal a horse that belonged to my brother. My brother followed them and returned later leading his horse. I heard still later that these two men were found shot dead in the woods. This was never discussed in our family."

"The Lord chooses his own agents from among mankind in his own mysterious way," said Reverend Hord, "even as he did on a street called Straight in Damascus. And it is not for mortal men to gainsay Him or His ways. You are young in years, Randolph Runnels, and your initiation period in this life has been painfully severe—yea, man is born to trouble as the sparks fly upward—but the training will be apt and suitable in the end, for the Lord has planned it so."

Reverend Hord dropped to his knees, a hand raised to shield his eyes. "Randolph Runnels, you have been a sinful man and the days of your atonement will be many and full of pain. You will feel the dark wings of death, but fear not. You shall not come to your grave until you are in a full age, like as a shock of corn cometh in its season. I see you offered a mission in a strange land . . . a long journey by water . . . a great river full of demons and monsters . . . a pestilence that walketh in darkness. . . ." Then the vision faded and Jesse Hord rose. "When the mission is offered, Brother Runnels, you must not refuse. To go is the Lord's will."

"From that time onward, my brother was a changed man," said Mrs. Marsden. "He abided under his own vine and fig tree at our family home on the Colorado River, ate his own grapes and drank from his own cistern. The saloons and gambling halls of San Antonio and Austin City knew him not."

For two years Randolph Runnels farmed the family acres and waited. The rifle and handguns, hanging from a peg on the wall by the rock fireplace, were taken down only to shoot game, or when owl hoots at dusk from the dark line of trees along the river held an ominously human quality. The news of the gold discovery in California swept through Texas late in 1849. Many of the settlers boarded up their cabins, packed their families and possessions and headed west. One group of men formed a company to ride to California on horseback, carrying their gear on pack animals. They hoped to reach the diggings fast, get their gold and be back with their families in Texas within a year. A delegation asked Randolph Runnels to lead the party. "He was not even faintly stirred by the proposal," said Mrs. Marsden.

It was not until the Howland and Aspinwall official appeared on his mule with his Isthmus proposal that Runnels stirred himself, packing his belongings for a long journey and kissing the tearful womenfolk goodby.

"And thus our brother left us," said Mrs. Marsden, "never to see his kith and kin nor his old home place again in this life. All at the behest of a stranger, because of a preacher's prophecy. But I know that I shall see him again on the Other Shore, where Mother and Father will dry every tear."

In 1851 when Runnels journeyed to Panama, there were five United States Mail Steam Line vessels plying regularly between New Orleans and Chagres—the *Alabama, Falcon, Mexico, Pacific* and *Philadelphia.* Eight other steamers operated from New York to Chagres. These 13 ships, boasting a total capacity of 5,000 passengers, were in constant movement to and from the Isthmus.

Runnels boarded the *Falcon,* the veteran of the Panama run. An 891-ton steamer built in 1848, she was a single-decker with a round stern and three masts. She had regular accommodations for 60 first-class passengers and 150 in the steerage, but during Gold Rush days she regularly carried at least 150 in the first-class cabins and 250 below decks, in addition to the crew. "We are crowded in very much like the Army transport to Vera Cruz during the war," Runnels wrote his mother. The main dining saloon of the *Falcon* was a long, narrow room extending two-thirds the length of the ship. The walls of the dining saloon were lined with the doors of the first-class cabins—tiny, crowded compartments. A long table, with a bench bolted to the deck on each side, ran the length of the dining room. Light and air entered through skylights and ventilators. Between meals the table was always crowded with passengers playing cards or writing letters.

The bulkheads and woodwork, once painted a soft gray, were now stained with greasy spots from lolling heads, and marred with the idle writings of those who had gone on before: names and addresses, humorous sayings and scraps of verse. The unswept deck was filthy with cigar butts, orange rinds and other garbage. The open deck was crowded still further by the pens of livestock. The lack of refrigeration made carrying livestock a necessity to provide the passengers with fresh meat. Stephen H. Branch, a correspondent for the New York *Herald* traveling to the Isthmus on the *Falcon,* described them: "Hens, sheep, goats, cattle and pigs—all destined to find their ways into the capacious pots of the galleys." In the early mornings of the voyage the passengers might be awakened by the crowing of roosters, and during the hot, windless days on the tropic sea they became used to the smell from the pens, which added its quality to the odor of coal smoke and unwashed humanity which enveloped the ship.

The nature of Runnels' mission set him apart from the other travelers. Their destination was California, while his was the Isthmus of Panama. They would push on to their dreams of finding golden hoards in California, while he would seek his destiny on the Yankee Strip. We see him, a small calm man, not unhandsome, walking alone and silent through the groups of excited Argonauts burdened with their money bags, miracle gold washers and unfamiliar weapons—a small man with an air of authority, journeying to the Isthmus on a dedicated mission.

The *Falcon* could approach to within only two miles of Chagres—a heavy sea was running under black clouds laced with bright tendrils of lightning. Runnels and his fellow passengers, crowded in the pitching longboats, neared the alien shore as thunder rumbled ominously behind the jungle-covered hills. Debarking at the railroad company dock, they went at once to the Irvine House to eat their first meal ashore and try to arrange transport to Panama City. They stared curiously at the crude signs of Yankee Chagres—"Jack of Clubs," "Davy Crockett," "House of All Nations"—the gambling halls, billiard parlors and brothels. Even though it was early in the day, most of the establishments were crowded with customers.

Through the influence of the railroad company agent at Yankee Chagres, Runnels obtained a prized seat in one of the new lifeboats of the Isthmus Transportation Company which had just begun service on the Chagres. This unique company had been formed by Captain Abraham Bunker, until recently shipping-news reporter of the New York *Herald.* The lifeboats, imported from New York and New Orleans, carried a dozen or more passengers and were easier to handle and offered a faster, more comfortable ride than the bungos.

On his way upriver Runnels saw his first live alligator—an ugly snout full of jagged teeth yawning suddenly from what appeared to be a gray log on the river bank. Truly it resembled one of the "monsters" mentioned in Jesse Hord's prophecy.

At Gorgona Runnels left the boat for the more familiar seat on a mule, "whose back was so narrow and sharp it almost cut up to the chin before the city of Panama was finally gained," Runnels wrote to his mother. His party met with no mishap on the jungle trail, but most of the members were apprehensive of outlaw attacks and test-fired their arms often to make sure they were in operating condition. "They expended almost as much powder and ball on the ride as Worth's Brigade during the siege of Vera Cruz," Runnels commented.

As darkness fell on the second day after leaving Gorgona, Runnels and his party entered the ancient gate of Panama City, the hoofs of their mules clicking on the cobblestone streets. After turning in the animals at the mule barns of Hurtado y Hermanos, the group scattered to seek lodgings. Runnels went at once to the American Hotel.

The post of United States Consul at Panama City was no sinecure during the Gold Rush period. William A. Nelson, the incumbent, was called upon to hear an endless variety of complaints, charges and countercharges in the controversies arising between passengers and representatives of the steamship and express companies. Nelson wielded power unknown to consuls of modern times. When charges were made by passengers against ship captains or express agents, he instituted inquiries and held hearings. When it was shown that the United States statutes had been violated, Nelson meted out the prescribed punishments. He could, and did on occasions, remove incompetent captains from their commands, levy fines, order mutinous sailors sent home in irons and force ship brokers and passenger agents to provide supplies and services necessary for the health and safety of their passengers.

A rotund, balding man whose countenance was pitted with smallpox scars, Nelson had been a resident of Panama City for years, surviving innumerable bouts with fever and other tropical afflictions. In addition to his official post as U. S. Consul, he was a successful businessman in his own right—a partner in the express firm of Zachrisson and Nelson—and a large landowner. He knew the Isthmus and its people as no other foreign resident. Now, during the stress and confusion brought on by the Gold Rush and the building of the railroad, he was the keystone of the small English-speaking community of the city and next to Governor Aniño was acknowledged to be the most powerful governmental official on Yankee Strip.

"The American council (*sic*) at Panama told Randolph of the unholy exploits of the highwaymen and murderers on the Isthmus and gave him a secret commission to punish them by any means whatsoever," reported Mrs. Marsden.

Runnels' orders were to enter the mule express business on the Isthmus and, while engaged in this "cover" occupation, secretly organize a force to wage war on the criminal element. These orders led to the founding of the vigilante group known to Panama history as the Isthmus Guard. During its brief history it injected a form of legalistic terror into life on the Isthmus—a terror directed mainly against the group known as the Derienni.

New express companies entered the field almost daily, so the appearance of another one did not excite curiosity. Small advertisements began appearing in the Isthmus newspapers: "Runnels Express Service. Panama-Gorgona or Ocean-to-Ocean. Prompt. R. Runnels, Prop."

Success in the express business on the Yankee Strip lay in obtaining pack animals. Mules were so scarce they were almost worth their weight in gold. Runnels, it appeared, had a gift for finding them. Soon his barns in Panama City and Gorgona were full of the snorting, cantankerous animals. Unknown to the general public, each major express carrier had donated animals to put him in business.

While Runnels was organizing his company, the Panama Railroad was continuing to flounder toward bankruptcy and Commodore Vanderbilt's attacks on the Panama Route became more flagrant. Taking advantage of the confusion on the New York docks, gangs of his agents accosted prospective passengers lined up in front of the U. S. Mail Steam Line office, offering lower fares, faster service and greater comforts. Vanderbilt's men warned of the cholera and mud on the Isthmus and described the crossing at Nicaragua as sheer joy, neglecting to mention the rain, the rock slides, the rapids on the San Juan River and the recurring revolutions. In addition to shortening the distance from the East Coast to San Francisco, the Nicaragua Route allegedly offered a cooler climate free from tropical diseases. This sounded good to those who heeded the horror stories of the Panama Route.

The rosy claims were not all borne out, however. Many of the travelers across Nicaragua found oppressive heat, swarms of insects, and ailments curiously similar to the malaria, yellow fever and cholera which supposedly did not exist there. Also, Vanderbilt had begun his service before facilities ashore were complete. As a result, many of his early travelers across the Transit experienced hardships which made those in Panama seem mild in comparison, and which inspired many complaints in newspapers.

In an attempt to quell the bad publicity, R. J. Vanderwater, Vanderbilt's new passenger agent at San Francisco, wrote this letter telling of his personal experiences on the Transit, which was published in the Panama *Star*, August 11, 1851:

"I was a passenger on the *Prometheus*, from New York, July 14 last. We reached San Juan del Norte on the 23rd; left there by the iron steamer, *Sir Henry L. Bulwer*, on the 24th; ran about 45 miles up the San Juan River; and came to anchor for the night. On the 26th, having walked around the portage (300 yards) we took bungos, ten miles to the Toro rapid, where we got on board the steamer *Director,* for Virgin Bay; arrived there at daylight Sunday, 27th, but finding no signal of the arrival of the steamship *Pacific* at San Juan del Sur, we passed up the lake ten miles, to the city of Rivas, a place of 10,000 inhabitants, where we remained until Thursday, and then came on board the *Pacific;* left San Juan on Friday, at 2 P. M. . . . Hereafter the ships and boats will meet regularly, and the passengers will pass over the Company's road to Virgin Bay, (12 miles and 18 chains) which is true, is now only a mule road, but it is being laid with plank, and will soon be a good wagon road. However, with all the obstacles incident to a first trip, I came from ocean to ocean, in exactly 40 hours running time. . . ."

Vanderwater had high praise for the hostelries on the route, especially the one at Rivas which he claimed "shames all Panama."

On September 7, 1851, the newspaper *Alta California* in San Francisco printed a letter from a Dr. Rabe who disagreed with Vanderwater's description of the Transit Route. Dr. Rabe too had been a passenger on the first voyage of the *Prometheus* to Greytown. He claimed that because of taking the Transit he had arrived in San Francisco fourteen days later than if he had gone via Panama. Regarding the facilities in Nicaragua, he said:

"As to the 'twelve mile road' that is coming—so is Christmas. As to the 'hotel at Rivas that shames all Panama'—it certainly shames the Devil. One more matter: people are not to be gulled now-a-days by 'forty running hours'; the time consumed in transit from point to point was five days; and we were not even encumbered by baggage."

Dr. Rabes version of transit hardships on his east-to-west crossing of Nicaragua in July of 1851 was supported by a round-robin letter signed by the passengers of a west-to-east crossing two months later—a crossing reminiscent of the melancholy experience of the Gordon's California Association two years before. "In the first place," stated the letter, "we were informed by Vanderwater, the agent of the line at San Francisco, that we would be put through in . . . twenty-two or three days . . . that we could cross the Isthmus (Nicaragua) in two or three days—that everything was arranged, and a good road."

On disembarking at San Juan del Sur, Vanderbilt's new port on the Pacific, they found no mules waiting to carry them the twelve miles to the lake. After waiting three days, they shouldered their luggage and hiked, finding the road rutted, muddy and almost impassable. They left the roadside strewn with belongings thrown away because they were too heavy to carry. At Rivas on Lake Nicaragua they waited six more days. When no steamer appeared, they hired native bungos and set out around the lake—"at the imminent danger of our lives." Five days later they arrived at San Carlos, the lake shore village at the origin of the San Juan River.

"We then started down the river," stated the round robin, "and we were compelled to row all night, and we got to Greytown in some thirty-six hours." At Greytown there was another shock. The Vanderbilt steamer on which their tickets were booked had not waited for them. It had sailed the day before, loaded with passengers who had preceded them across the Transit. The late-arrivals could either wait for the *Prometheus,* whose return was scheduled several weeks in the future, or buy tickets at their own expense on another steamer.

Although no fevers were recognized to exist on the Transit Route, a malady with all the symptoms of cholera was in epidemic stages in Greytown. Because of this epidemic most of the passengers chose to pay their own passage to New York on the steamer of an independent line which happened to be in the harbor. The Vanderbilt agent at Greytown refused to return to them the cost of the unused portions of their tickets. "Wait for the return of the *Prometheus,*" he counseled.

"But we may die of cholera in the meantime," they said.

"There is no cholera in Greytown or anywhere on the Transit Route," said the agent sternly.

Those who took the steamer of the independent line arrived in New York 45 days after leaving San Francisco. Many of those who waited for the *Prometheus* are still there, buried in the British cemetery at Greytown. Whatever it was that resembled cholera killed them. Vanderbilt's agent also returned home on the *Prometheus*. For several days prior to the arrival of the steamer he had been confined to his room with a fever. On the fourth day he rose from his bed, perfectly rational, dressed himself and went to the barber. The Indian barber lathering his face said, "The soap dries as fast as I put it on your face." He then told the agent to make his peace with God because he had a fatal case of fever. The agent laughed and went to the market, where he bought some fruit and returned to his room. "Shortly thereafter," wrote the British surgeon at Greytown, "he expired in a torrent of black vomit." His body, pickled in a hogshead, was returned to New York on the *Prometheus* for burial.

The last paragraph of the round-robin letter held this warning for those considering taking passage to California:

"And we here invoke the traveling community, if they value comfort, health, convenience and life, touch not the unclean thing, but deal with honorable men, who, if you are detained, will indemnify you, as they have heretofore done, by paying you a reasonable amount."

Vanderbilt countered with handbills and broadsides carrying such headlines as "Cholera on the Panama Route!" or "Robbed and Murdered on a Panama Trail!" The last gave lurid details of an outlaw raid on a gold train. "Hordes of villainous cutthroats run unchecked on the jungle trails," reported the handbill. "Robbery, Murder and unspeakable acts of Violence and Rapine are everyday occurrences on the Panama Route." But Vanderbilt and his associates in Nicaragua, as well as the "villainous cutthroats" in Panama, were unaware of an important fact—Randolph Runnels had arrived on the Yankee Strip.

The Runnels Express Service, "Panama-Gorgona or Ocean-to-Ocean," was now operating. Approximately 40 of the employees of this company were sworn into the secret organization called the Isthmus Guard. This was an era when secret organizations were widespread among American men. They were fascinated by "lodges" with cabalistic oaths and secret rituals, especially those dedicated to exacting violent retribution from evil-doers.

Runnels' men were a mixed crew of Yankees, Chileans, Peruvians, Mexicans and other individuals whose true nationality was difficult to classify. Fluent in "border" Spanish, Runnels had no difficulty in communicating with them. Between trips along the trail, he and his men hung about the cantinas and plazas of Panama, Gorgona, Cruces and Yankee Chagres, listening to gossip and identifying known highwaymen.

Because the actions of the bandits were so flagrant, identifying them was not difficult for people conversant in Spanish and the ways of the Isthmus. In his office behind his mule barn in Panama City, Runnels received messages from his agents and wrote down names and descriptions in a big black ledger which he kept locked in his safe. In this book he was compiling a secret list of individuals regularly engaged in violent crime on the Strip.

Meanwhile the robberies went unchecked. Guns would bark in the jungle and the next day mules without riders or packs would turn up at Gorgona or Cruces. The Derienni massacred boatloads of travelers on the Chagres and looted their dead bodies. Buzzards wheeled in the skies above the green jungle, marking the endings of these little dramas.

Runnels spent most of his days and evenings gambling with local businessmen at the La Vista Hotel—a known Derienni hangout in Panama City—and racing his fleet, blooded horses at the Juan Franco race track.

The highwaymen harassed the gold trains with such impunity that several of the large shippers spoke seriously of transferring their business to the Transit Route where Commodore Vanderbilt promised to hire units of the Nicaraguan army as guards.

Consul Nelson sent Runnels a two-word, unsigned message. "Strike soon," the message said.

There was a night early in 1852 when the horse stalls of the Runnels Express Service all were empty. From ocean to ocean during that night, in Cruces, Gorgona, and Panama City, men were arrested in saloons, gambling houses, brothels and imposing residences. Their captors were masked and made no explanation for their actions.

The Isthmus Guard hanged the entire group—37 in all—on the inner side of the sea wall known as the East Battery, where the Argonauts liked to stroll.

Next morning crowds gathered to stare at the dangling bodies. Monroe Polter, a lawyer from New York en route to California who witnessed the spectacle that morning, reported: "It seemed to be a democratic hanging, as all races on the Isthmus were represented." Certainly the Guard had not drawn class lines. The bodies of several wealthy and prominent businessmen dangled in the breeze alongside those of highwaymen.

Hugo Elfenbein, another traveler, reported in a letter to his wife in Boston: "It is said to be the work of a local vigilance committee headed by a Texan named Runnells (*sic*). No explanations are offered, and I hasten to say, no questions have been asked. Silently the citizens survey the appalling spectacle and then go on about their business."

That the executions were evidence of divine retribution was the opinion of many of the American onlookers. "The Lord rained upon Sodom and Gomorrah brimstone and fire," wrote one. "This is an omen of the wrath to come."

Years later, Charity Marsden commented upon the affair as it related to the character of her brother. "Before enlisting in the good cause of Christianity, my brother went about like Goliath of Gath, full of heaven-defying wickedness, to defy the hosts of God's conquering army. He suffered a similar defeat. After his conversion, like Saul of Tarsus, he breathed out threatenings and slaughter and made havoc."

Runnels' havoc on the Isthmus, however, brought sudden peace. Most of the ringleaders of the Derienni had been eliminated at one stroke. The trails grew quiet. The gold trains traveled through the steamy jungle undisturbed by any noise except the chattering of the monkeys and the raucous voices of the parrots.

The employees of Runnels Express Service carried their share of freight and in their spare time still frequented the bars and gambling halls of the Isthmus. Standing on the docks at Panama City and Yankee Chagres, they scrutinized new arrivals closely. Occasionally they selected names from passenger manifests and reported them to Runnels for marking down in his big ledger.

William Nelson and the other businessmen on the Strip were confident that the mainspring of crime on the Isthmus had been broken. The Wells Fargo agent wrote his New York office expressing this view and gave himself a light pat on the back by saying this benign situation had been brought about by "instituting actions in which your obedient servant played a part."

Runnels was not so optimistic about the future. "There are at least fifty men still at large on the Isthmus who have engaged in murder and banditry in the past," he wrote Consul Nelson, "and there is no reason to believe they will not do so again because a leopard does not change his spots nor a tiger his stripes."

VIII

The Familiar Toot

As 1851 NEARED ITS END, A PERSISTENT RUMOR BEGAN MAKING THE rounds of Wall Street that George Law was weakening and would soon make a deal with Vanderbilt to allow U. S. Mail steamers to discharge passengers at San Juan del Norte as well as Chagres. This would indeed be a blow to the Panama Route. Then, unexpectedly, human curiosity rescued them.

In mid-December of 1851 two of Law's steamers, the *Georgia* and the *Philadelphia,* arrived off Chagres during a violent storm. After sacrificing several lives attempting to land passengers in longboats, both steamers turned down the coast to weather the storm in Navy Bay. When the winds finally abated and the ships made ready to return to Chagres, the passengers suddenly heard the familiar toot of a locomotive whistle and saw a train of gondola cars move across the causeway from Manzanillo Island and disappear into the jungle with the puffing smoke from the locomotive smokestack marking its passage inland. It was the daily work train carrying laborers to cut back undergrowth and replace washed-out ties on the completed section of the line. The ships' passengers immediately clamored to ride the train and sent a delegation to Colonel Totten seeking permission.

Totten was not disposed to grant the request. He had no passenger coaches nor any instructions from company headquarters telling him what rates to charge. The passengers were insistent, saying they would pay whatever fare he asked. Totten thought the matter over. To institute passenger service now, he felt, would be premature; it would delay completion of the line. Intending to discourage the would-be riders, Totten quoted an exorbitant fare of 50 cents a mile each, plus three dollars per 100 pounds for luggage. He had grossly underestimated the virulence of the gold fever. Practically all 1,100 passengers eagerly paid and scrambled into the gondolas. By the day's end they had been transported to Gatun, and Totten had collected almost $7,000 in United States currency.

The response from New York to this news was enthusiastic. George Law ordered his steamers to stop at Manzanillo instead of Yankee Chagres. The railroad company rushed down passenger coaches. Trains met every steamer and the seven miles of track began to yield an unbelievable revenue. The good news reached Wall Street and the bulls charged into Panama Railroad stock, pushing the price of shares up and up. When the company directors offered a new issue to raise $4,000,000 needed to complete construction, it sold magically. The impetus of high hopes and new capital pushed the tracks forward across the soggy terrain of the Chagres valley toward Lion Hill and Bohío Soldado.

George Law, rescued from the humiliation of dickering with Vanderbilt for a passenger concession in Nicaragua, saw his large holdings of Panama Railroad stock soar in value. Convinced now that Panama would emerge victorious in the struggle with the other routes, Law entered the affray in earnest, offering to construct docks and wharf facilities on the two oceans at such a low cost that the railroad company could not refuse.

At Manzanillo Law built a wharf 1,000 feet long and 40 feet wide with a tin roof, coppering the underwater pilings to protect them from the teredo worm. Behind the wharf he built a warehouse of native stone, 300 feet long by 80 feet wide. And on the extreme seaward point of the island, west of the port entrance, he mounted an iron lighthouse, 60 feet high, with the brightest available Fresnel light. Ship captains could then breathe more easily as they approached the treacherous coast during stormy weather.

When the steamers stopped unloading passengers at the mouth of the Chagres, the boatmen moved upriver to Gatun, and the ramshackle town of Yankee Chagres disappeared from the face of the earth. The green jungle swallowed the town site; the wharf decayed, fell into the sea and was washed away. Today no trace of Yankee Chagres exists.

The town on Manzanillo Island, still without a formal name, was generally called "Otro Lado"—"the other side"—by residents of Panama City, or sometimes "Aspinwall" in honor of the founder of the Panama Railroad Company. Even for the tropics it was a pest hole. There was no sewage disposal system or means of drainage; garbage and refuse were dumped into the streets. Privies hung over the water on the ends of the piers and docks. Since the ebb and flow of the tides never carried the waste far to sea, a vast foggy stink hung constantly over the town.

H. H. Bancroft described the town as it was in 1851:

"Travel the world over and in every place you may find something better than is found in any other place. Searching for the specialty in which Aspinwall excelled, we found it in her carrion birds, which cannot be surpassed in size or smell. Manzanillo Island may boast of the finest vultures on the planet. Originally a swamp, the foundations of the buildings were below the level of the ocean, and dry land was made by filling in as occasion required. The result in this soft soil made of filth and vegetable putridity may be imagined. The very ground on which one trod was pregnant with disease, and death was distilled in every breath of air. . . . Glued furniture falls to pieces; leather molds, and iron oxidizes in twenty-four hours."

For years the town lacked a convenient source of fresh water, other than rain. Ultimately the railroad company laid a pipe from the Chagres at Gatun to bring water, but prior to its completion, the residents had to depend on open-topped wooden tanks—called "catch" basins—placed on the roofs of buildings. These had to catch enough water during the rainy season to tide the town over the four-month dry period. Many building owners kept live fish in the tanks as an easily accessible food supply. Some tried to keep the water clean, but most allowed the "catch" basins to become murky aquariums full of tadpoles, frogs and serpentine water plants. This water was peddled in the street from jars and bottles. No wonder everyone suffered from intestinal complaints and that a cholera epidemic was an annual occurrence.

Truly, "Death was distilled in every breath of air," as Bancroft said. The residents saw death daily and grew calloused to it. Death came not only from disease, but from violence. The corpses of murdered men were found each morning lying in the gutters or floating face down in the bay. Since the railroad company owned the place, the company had to dispose of the bodies. Many of them—stripped of all clothing—were hopelessly unidentifiable. These corpses, like those of the anonymous dead railroad workers, were pickled and sold to the medical schools. The traffic in cadavers, although an extremely profitable sideline for the railroad company, was not a species of success to which the officials ever admitted publicly.

In an attempt to avoid fever and dysentery, railroad officials and businessmen of Manzanillo sometimes went on regimens of champagne doused heavily with quinine. This was supposed to be an effective cure for tropical affliction, but when pursued too long the practice brought delirium tremens and other symptoms as deadly as the fever itself.

Everyone, residents and travelers alike, cursed the tropical rain—averaging more than 11 feet annually. But the rain was a blessing to the tinderbox town, reducing as it did the number of fires. During the dry season flames gutted the town on several occasions. These widespread fires contributed greatly to the death rate, but unlike simple murder generally rendered the corpses unsuitable for commercial export.

The best hotels on Manzanillo were the Howard, the City and

the Aspinwall. Beds cost three dollars a day. A dozen other hotels and rooming houses offered lower rates. Travelers were wise to elicit definite commitments as to price in advance, because some unscrupulous innkeepers would present exorbitant bills just prior to the travelers' departure and attempt to extort payment by impounding their luggage.

The railroad, the port and the hotels—with their allied interests—were Manzanillo's principal businesses, but these were closely followed by another interlocking threesome: the hospital, the barbershops and the houses of prostitution.

The barbers doubled as undertakers, charging the hospital embalming and pickling fees. While live patrons were being clipped and shaved in front of the shop, they could hear the hammering of carpenters building coffins and barrels in the rear. Many barbers were also active as clap doctors, prescribing their nostrums for both the girls and the patrons they infected.

Most of the prostitutes worked in filthy stalls along a narrow muddy thoroughfare called Bottle Alley. The pimps stood outside in ankle-deep mud to hawk the claims of their lovelies and to propel drunks bodily through the swinging doors of the stalls. The consumption of alcohol along this street was considered unusually large even for the Yankee Strip. Over the years liquor bottles tossed into the street created a solid layer of glass beneath the mud. In the 1890's pavement-laying contractors found it unnecessary to put down a gravel foundation because the thousands of bottles buried there served the purpose.

The girls came in all colors: Negroes, Caucasians, Orientals, and exotic mixtures of many races. Health laws were unknown and prophylactics had not been invented. As a result, a large percentage of the prostitutes presented their customers with gonorrhea, syphilis, and Phthirius pubis, the crab louse. Refined people never discussed these matters. Prostitution was a taboo subject in the press and the only medical group deeply concerned with venereal disease was the United States Army Medical Service. Army cures then prescribed for gonorrhea were "sulphate of zinc, alkaline mixes, cubebs, injection of a weak solution of nitrate of silver every two hours and Epsom Salts." The best known treatment for syphilis was to daub the chancre with mercury ointment.

Many a dallying wayfarer across the Yankee Strip arrived in California with a deadly late-blooming blossom. A San Francisco doctor wrote his drug supplier in New York: "The macaronis and whoremongers of the Isthmus are sending us more patients than we can minister to. In addendum to the drugs ordered under this same cover, please send me any book or treatise you can find relating to cures for clap and the soft chancre."

The whores came from the world over. Earnings of ordinary prostitutes were especially low in England. During the eighteenth century, we are told, Boswell never paid more than a sixpence for a brief encounter, and a century later the price had not risen. It is no wonder that the lure of gold brought many London pimps and their whores to the Isthmus in the steerages of the British steamers. The fair-skinned girls were very popular but unfortunately short-lived, being especially susceptible to fever.

The girls and their pimps—"Buttock and Twang" as they were called in the cockney jargon—slept most of the day and commenced their business as soon as darkness fell. The Buttock made the approach and fulfilled her part of the contract leaning back spread-eagled against a building wall. While her client performed, she picked his pocket. The Twang stood by with drawn dirk, ready to give assistance. If the client seemed well-heeled, the Buttock signaled and the Twang leaped forward and struck with his dirk. Then he and the girl dragged the dead man away to rifle his pockets and money belt at their leisure.

But the city had its more respectable occasions. On February 29, 1852, the railroad company laid the cornerstone of a new passenger station and office building, the first brick structure on the island. The ceremony brought railroad officials, members of consular staffs, local businessmen, and others. Among the dignitaries were George Law, John L. Stephens, Minor C. Story—a large railroad construction contractor—and a local resident whose name is listed in the record only as R. Webb of Manzanillo Island. During the attendant celebration the town was given a formal name.

Dr. Victoriano de Diego Paredes, a Colombian official recently designated Minister to the United States, made the principal address. The diplomat praised the spirit of Anglo-Latin friendship that was supposedly prevailing in the town and lauded the energy and technical ability of the officials of the railroad company. He prophesied that the town on Manzanillo would become "the commercial emporium of the Americas and perhaps the whole world." Then he proposed that "we call this town 'Aspinwall,' as a slight homage to so respectable a person."

R. Webb accepted the name on behalf of the local citizens, the one recorded event of his life.

John L. Stephens, in a brief speech, said, "No name could have been selected more proper, or which would give more general satisfaction." It is not unreasonable to suspect that Stephens had prompted the Colombian diplomat to suggest Aspinwall's name for the town.

Dr. Paredes placed in the cornerstone a copper box containing a document describing the ceremony, a copy of the New York *Herald* of February 9, 1852, and a coin from each of the following countries: the United States, France, Great Britain and New Granada.

The railroad company directors immediately sent out notices to the world that the town on Manzanillo was now formally named Aspinwall. Postal guides were amended; charts were changed by writing in that name, and the matter seemed settled. Then the central government of the Colombian Confederation at Bogotá objected. Bogotá repudiated Paredes' name suggestion and issued an order naming the town for the original discoverer of Manzanillo, Christopher Columbus. The name of the town was not Aspinwall, said Bogotá; the true name of the town was Colón.

The Panama Railroad directors refused to change the name. The company had built the town, they said, and should have the privilege of naming it. Not so, said Bogotá. Manzanillo and all of Panama was still under the sovereignty of Colombia. The name of the town was Colón! Latin pride and Yankee stubbornness met head on. "You may call the city what you please," the directors wrote to Bogotá, "but we are going to call it Aspinwall and that name will appear on all city buildings, including the railroad station."

Confusion resulted. For years mail came addressed to "Aspinwall," "Colón," "Aspinwall-Colón," or "Colón-Aspinwall." The town's name varied widely on maps and charts. The confusion existed until 1890 when the government at Bogotá ordered its post office department to return all mail to sender addressed with the name "Aspinwall" on the envelope. Rather than interrupt the flow of mail, the railroad bowed to the Bogotá government and grudgingly accepted the name Colón. Thus it remains to this day.

The political, social, commercial and sinful activities on Manzanillo went on without the participation of James L. Baldwin, Totten's energetic field superintendent. His sphere lay in the wilderness, from the end of the rails onward, as far onward as he could hike and survey. From Gatun Baldwin plotted the course of the tracks along the base of an irregular line of highlands rising from the eastern side of the valley of the Chagres. Then the line struck the Gatun River and it was necessary to build a 97-foot bridge. While the bridge was being built, Baldwin scouted the route beyond the river, busily directing gangs in clearing underbrush, but finding time also to scribble observations in his notebook.

"The jungle here is like a green wall," wrote Baldwin, "and from high ground can be seen on the left two conical peaks—Lion and Tiger Hills—also covered with dense foliage."

These hills were named by the railroad construction crews because their monkey population filled the nights with a roaring sound that was at first mistaken for the sounds of lions and tigers. Baldwin marked the Lion Hill location on his map as a spot for a railroad way station and pushed on. Beyond Lion Hill the vegetation was less dense and more swamplike: large patches of cane, huge tree ferns, scrubby palms and mangroves rising out of dark pools of water. Here he observed the rare orchid—Peristera elata—known from the Spanish era on the Isthmus as "Flor del Espiritu Santo." The pure white blossom, almost tulip-like in shape, gave out a perfume similar to that of the magnolia. Within the cup lay what appeared to be the prone figure of an amazingly lifelike dove. The wings hung gracefully at the sides and the head bent forward so that the tiny red-tipped bill almost touched the breast. "Indeed, it seemed to be Nature's own portrayal of meek, ethereal innocence," wrote Baldwin. Dr. F. N. Otis in his railroad company history commented upon this orchid's beauty saying: "No wonder that early Catholics, ever on the alert for a phenomenon upon which to fasten the idea of a miraculous origin, should have named it for the Holy Ghost."

Baldwin pushed on to the projected location of the next way station, Ahorca Lagarto—"Hang the Lizard"—on the banks of the Chagres. The village name was of ancient origin. In 1549 the Spanish viceroy at Panama City had sent a military regiment of the Order of Santiago to clean out native insurgents in the interior. The regimental insignia emblazoned on the banners, helmets and breastplates of the troops was the figure of a lizard. This regiment camped one night on the Chagres near a small Indian village several miles above Gatun. During the early hours of the morning, frenzied natives attacked the Spanish troops, shouting the battle cry, "Ahorca Lagarto!"—Hang the lizard! The regiment was decimated. Only a few were able to hack their way through the attackers and escape in the jungle. Three centuries later this village was still called Ahorca Lagarto in memory of this attack. Under this name it became a station on the Panama Railroad.

Here was an area of the huge cedar trees from whose trunks the natives carved their large bungos. Baldwin noted that "the broad, plane-shaped roots stood like buttresses" and that the trunks towered up "as much as a hundred feet without a single branch to the capping canopy of foliage that was often fifty yards in diameter."

Baldwin located the spot for his station a short distance from a favorite tree of John L. Stephens. This was a giant cedar, larger even than its fellows, over six yards in diameter at the base. For years this tree—called "Stephens' Tree"—was pointed out to travelers on the Panama Railroad as a sight of local interest. There is a legend on the Isthmus surviving to this day that John L. Stephens died and was buried beneath this tree, but there is no truth in the story.

A mile or so beyond Ahorca Lagarto, James Baldwin saw with amazement what appeared to be the ruins of an ancient, lost city. He saw sections of wall, fortifications, watch towers, tall columns and Gothic arches, all overgrown with clinging green vines. Coming closer he saw that nature had created this illusion with parasitic bindweed which Baldwin termed "convolvuli." The trailing, twining growth had transformed rows of tall trees into solid barriers of green that resembled walls. Tall stumps of palms, overgrown with verdure, became broken classic columns. Where the tops of two trees leaned together to share the weight of the enveloping bindweed, a great Gothic arch was formed. The "ruins" extended for acres. Many were covered with huge blue trumpet-shaped flowers, similar to the morning-glory, which swayed constantly in the sluggish breeze.

After describing these wonders in his notebook, Baldwin continued his march up the Chagres valley, keeping the river on his right and a row of densely wooded hills to his left. At the base of these hills on the east bank of the Chagres was the village of Bohío Soldado—"Soldiers Home"—which he marked on his map as the next way station. Here a fine view of the river opened up. Just beyond Bohío was the freestone quarry utilized by the railroad for construction fill. Heretofore the crushed rock had been sent downriver to the sea on scows and flatboats and then towed along the coast of Manzanillo. When the rock quarry became accessible to the railroad itself, construction along the entire line of track could be quickened. Farther on, where the river bank steepened, was the site of John L. Stephens' cottage. Here Stephens had written the books describing his travels in Central America, Chiapas, and Yucatan, the carefree travels done in the days of his youth before he became involved in the business of railroad building.

The tracks reached Bohío Soldado in early March of 1852. On March 15 the company began a regular passenger schedule from Manzanillo to Bohío. Fare was five dollars a passenger and luggage was extra. From there the passengers continued upriver to Gorgona and Cruces by bungo boat.

Beyond Bohío the Chagres valley twisted like a snake, generally southeastward. The railroad track, following the east bank, cut straight across from the bend at Bohío to the bend at Buena Vistita. The latter was the usual native village of bamboo huts thatched with palm leaves and built on bare earthen floors. The natives here, noted Baldwin, were a mixture of Spanish and Indian, with only a few Negroes. The women stood stolidly in their long flounced muslin dresses, many carrying naked babies on their hips. The men were neither friendlier nor more hostile than "the usual native riffraff," Baldwin wrote. The refuse-littered area between the huts was a "hodgepodge of dogs, pigs, chickens and native children." All the humans—men, women and children—smoked the inevitable cigars.

The tracks reached Frijoles, another ancient native village, on May 1, 1852. Scouting in the neighborhood, Baldwin saw many scarlet and purple passion flowers growing, and in the trees "a vast number of oriole nests, beautifully woven and two or three feet long." The trees were vibrant with birds, their calls blending into a constant cacophony of sweet and discordant sound. Doves cooed and turpiales whistled sonorously. Baldwin observed that the turpiale was a bird about the size of a robin, with black and yellow plumage, "like a magpie in intelligence and cunning." In common with all travelers on the Isthmus, he was amazed by the toucan, a dark bird with scarlet breast about the size of a pigeon, owning a heavy serrated bill six or seven inches long. The bird fed itself in a most curious way, picking up food on the point of its beak by a sudden jerk, tossing it more than a foot into the air and catching it in its gaping mouth as it came down. In drinking, the bird made more extraordinary motions, bobbing its head up and down and side to side to gulp each mouthful. The Spanish priests said the toucan made the sign of the cross with its beak when it drank. They called the bird "Dios te de"—"God gives it to thee." When told this by the natives, Baldwin wrote, "More Popish tomfoolery."

The forest abounded in tapirs, monkeys, possums, anteaters, peccaries, sloths, deer, bear, and "two or three varieties of tiger cat." The iguanas, three to six feet in length, were eagerly sought by the natives. Baldwin tasted the cooked flesh and found it "tender and delicate as chicken." But he was revolted by the native practice of catching a female iguana, cutting her open to remove the eggs, and then allowing her to escape. A village priest assured Baldwin that the female iguana almost invariably recovered. The eggs, Baldwin noted, "had the appearance of yellow, shriveled marbles." Another denizen highly prized as food was the land crab, "light blue in color and large as half a coconut." Baldwin was astounded at their rapacity; the carcasses of dead or wounded large animals could be reduced to stripped skeletons in the course of a single night under their onslaught.

The insects were worrisome—tarantulas; centipedes; scorpions; white, red and black ants; mosquitoes; sand flies; fleas; wood ticks called garapatos; and chiggers. The chiggers were subtle in their attack, burrowing under the skin and depositing eggs which if not speedily removed would hatch a nest of minute worms, producing a great inflammation.

Venomous snakes were not common, Baldwin learned with surprise. Boa constrictors were seen occasionally—12 to 18 feet in length—but could be easily avoided. In fact they were quite man-shy, being eagerly hunted by the natives as food. The plentiful alligators in the rivers were not considered very dangerous to grown people, although they occasionally attacked dogs, cattle and small children.

In May of 1852, while Baldwin scouted the route beyond Frijoles, a contingent of French laborers came to Bohío Soldado to work as section hands. Shortly after their arrival they suddenly mutinied. Dropping their tools, they hoisted the tricolor of France over the new station house, and sang "La Marseillaise." The Irish section foreman was unable to find out what the problem was, because the laborers refused to discuss it in any language save French.

Baldwin was off somewhere in the wilderness, but President Stephens was visiting at his cottage nearby. The section foreman sent a locomotive speeding to seek his aid. With Stephens in the cab the locomotive backed all the way to Bohío. The sight of the French flag flying over the station irritated the railroad company president. "Take down that flag!" he shouted in English.

The leader of the French group, speaking in his own native tongue, advised Stephens that his men had grievances that had to be discussed in French only. Stephens, though he could speak French, shook his head. All company business had to be discussed in English, and the tricolor had to be replaced with the Stars and Stripes. When the stubborn Frenchmen made no move to comply, Stephens climbed back into the locomotive and returned to his cottage. He sent orders to the commissary at Manzanillo to send no food to the section gang at Bohío until they lowered the French flag and remembered their English.

Next day, a few hours after the daily ration train failed to appear, the engineer of a passing train noted that the Stars and Stripes again flew on the pole at Bohío station and that the French laborers were going about their work on the tracks. Stephens sent word to the commissary to deliver rations as scheduled the next day. There was no further work stoppage, but the French stubbornly refused to explain what had prompted their mutiny in the first place. Stephens prudently let the matter rest. The company officials never learned what had caused the short-lived uprising.

Leaving Frijoles, the tracks ran across a broad savanna and arrived at Tabernilla on May 30, 1852. In June the work began to be slowed by the advent of the rainy season. Then cholera struck the Isthmus, the worst epidemic in years. By the end of June the disease had taken such toll that construction work stopped completely a mile short of Barbacoas.

The islands of Panama Bay: Taboga, Flamenco, Islaño, Calebra and Perico. (Drawing by Dr. F. N. Otis)

Culebra (Summit) in 1854 when the tracks stopped there. (Drawing by Dr. F. N. Otis)

U. S. Mail Steam Line docks at Aspinwall circa 1855.
(Drawing by Dr. F. N. Otis)

Camels as pack animals on the Isthmus during the 1850's; a short-lived experiment.

IX

The Mad Hatter's March

MEDICAL PRACTITIONERS TODAY KNOW MUCH OF THE NATURE OF cholera: an acute, infectious and contagious disease affecting specifically the terminal ileum of the small intestine. The germs enter the human body through the mouth. An impure water supply is the principal source of infection, but food that has been contaminated by flies, cockroaches, or rats and mice which have acquired the bacilli from contact with human feces is also important in spreading the disease. Even today, with the best of hospital care, the death rate is 20 to 50 per cent.

After the ingestion of tainted food or water, the incubation period within the body may be only a few hours or as long as five days. The average time is three days. The symptoms are always the same. A sudden cramp strikes the belly with a violent kick, bending the victim double. Retching and vomiting become uncontrollable. A constant diarrhea begins; the body, gradually dehydrated, shrinks to a fantastic degree. The skin becomes dry, wrinkled and very cool, and body temperature may fall as low as 75 degrees Fahrenheit. Most deaths occur during the first 24 hours of this cold or "algid" stage.

The face of the victim takes on a shrunken, anxious expression and his eyes stare straight ahead glassily, because his eyelids cannot close. If he survives the algid stage, but does not rally strongly, he will die on the fifth or sixth day from uremia due to complete failure of the kidney function.

American doctors of the 1850's had had ample opportunity to observe cholera. In 1849 a huge epidemic had swept the Eastern Seaboard, killing thousands. During that year Dr. John Snow, in London, demonstrated how the disease was communicated by water, but his discovery was not widely publicized in American medical circles. Doctors of the time held diverse and conflicting theories about the cause and transmittal of cholera. Some believed the source was "putrid animal poison." In those days the sight of dead livestock lying unburied was common, especially in the crowded city slums, and the carcasses were suspected to be disease sources because of the stink, if for no other reason. Other doctors believed cholera and other fevers arose from "the miasma from swamps and bogs." The "miasma" theory was the one most held on the Isthmus, mainly because there were so many swamps and bogs.

Certain egotists believed that the disease attacked only those "whose blood was poorly-organized"—the poverty-stricken, the dissolute, the unhealthy or the cowardly. Subscribers to this notion were convinced that well-fed, confident, fearless people escaped the infection. Because cholera was prevalent among southern Negroes, one learned medical man deduced: "The Negro is more susceptible because he has more nitrogen and less oxygen about his person than a white man."

Remedies varied as widely as the theories. Doctors prescribed alcoholic spirits, generally wine, as well as camphor, tincture of rhubarb, laudanum and opium. They administered mustard plasters or hot baths to offset the temperature decline of the algid stage, and devised ferocious purges—calomel and enemas of hot salt water and tobacco juice—to exorcise the demon from the patient's body. They believed that heavy consumption of hard spirits—whiskey, brandy, gin and rum—lowered one's resistance to cholera, but that drinking moderate quantities of light wine and beer combated the disease. In the midst of all the confusion and ignorance the doctors of the era *did* know two things about cholera: the dreaded symptoms, and the almost inevitable outcome.

In April of 1852 the United States Secretary of War laid down the beginnings of a tragedy when he sent orders transferring the 4th Infantry Regiment from the Eastern Seaboard to California, via the Isthmus of Panama, as a military garrison for the newly acquired West Coast territory. The orders authorized the regimental members to take their wives and children with them at government expense. "We were wild to go," wrote Delia Sheffield, wife of a sergeant in Company H. The gold fever had attacked the military as well as the civilian. Many of the soldiers confided that they intended to desert as soon as they landed in California and disappear into the gold diggings.

Due to the physical disabilities of age and acute alcoholism Colonel William Whistler, the regimental commander, was replaced by Lieutenant Colonel Benjamin Louis Eulalie Bonneville, the second-in-command. Bonneville had a legendary name with the general public as an explorer of the Far West, but was not generally respected by his military colleagues. Small of stature, vain and excitable in disposition, Bonneville was a unique personality even for the Army of that era. On his bald head he always wore a tall white beaver hat instead of the regulation headgear. His troops, who despised him, were always shouting from cover, "Where did you get that hat?" His crude manners toward his subordinates and their families also brought him much criticism. Eunice Tripler, wife of Captain Charles S. Tripler, the regimental surgeon, described Bonneville caustically, if redundantly, in her memoirs as "a very stupid man mentally."

Bonneville had spent most of his military career on exploring expeditions in charge of small, informal and loosely organized commands. He had not been forced by long periods of garrison duty as a young officer to learn the social amenities. While his colleagues were learning to bow and scrape at garrison soirées and receptions, he had lived in the wilderness of the Far West with Indians, trappers and Long Hunters.

The new commander immediately made it known that several of his staff officers were personally obnoxious to him, particularly First Lieutenant U. S. Grant, the regimental quartermaster, familiarly addressed as "Sam" Grant by his contemporaries. "It was something that had occurred in Mexico," Lieutenant Henry C. Hodges wrote later in an attempt to explain Bonneville's animosity toward Grant.

The "something" in Mexico was one of the several embarrassing incidents which dogged Grant's career as a junior officer. In 1848, not long after being appointed quartermaster, Grant was entrusted with $1,000 in regimental funds. Not having a strongbox, he put the money in a locked trunk owned by his friend Captain John Gore. This trunk was kept under a bunk in quarters occupied by Gore and Lieutenant Henry D. Wallen, another friend of Grant's. At Jalapa, Mexico, someone broke the trunk lock while Gore and Wallen were asleep and stole the money. The subsequent investigation failed to incriminate Grant, Gore or Wallen, but it did reveal that all three had been drinking on the night of the theft. Heavy drinking was commonplace in the Army of that day; few members of any board of inquiry could condemn the embarrassing results of a spree too sternly without eliciting criticism of some escapade of their own. Grant was exonerated, but for years the loss of the money preyed on his mind. He felt it was the source of many veiled innuendoes.

Bonneville mistrusted Grant as a result of the loss and was rankled further that his partners in the affair, Gore and Wallen, were still regimental officers. It is not clear at this time whether Bonneville wanted Grant removed from the regiment completely or merely removed from the staff to a post in one of the line companies. In any case, he did begin a campaign to remove him as quartermaster and in so doing ran headlong into the formidable opposition of Captain Charles S. Tripler, the regimental surgeon.

The veteran Tripler had the reputation of being a firebrand.

Although he and Grant were close friends, it taxes the imagination to conceive of two individuals contrasting more in personality and appearance. Grant was small in stature, clean-shaven, quiet-spoken and self-effacing. Tripler was tall, bearded, aggressive in demeanor and given to oracular pronouncements.

Tripler's objections caused such a stir among the other officers that Bonneville dropped his move to replace Grant. It must be said that some of the officers agreed with their commander's low opinion of the quartermaster.

In 1852 Grant was 29 years old, a thin, rather moody young man whose dislike for military discipline and routine increased as he grew older. His first eight-year enlistment had been up the previous July. After a period of fretful indecision he re-enlisted. Since his wife was pregnant when the West Coast orders came, Grant decided that she should not make the trip at that time, but follow later.

The regiment began assembling at Governor's Island, New York, in May 1852. Because the unit was under strength, the War Department authorized the enlistment of recruits. Dr. Tripler reported 243 new men were received and examined on June 23, and 150 more on July 3. The prospect of a free ocean voyage to the gold fields gave great impetus to recruiting. By the time the regiment sailed, it numbered more than 600 soldiers and "over a hundred wives, children and camp followers."

Dr. Tripler, in the course of arranging for shipment of his medical supplies, was informed by officials of the Panama Railroad Company that an epidemic of cholera had recently broken out on the Isthmus. Tripler went at once to tell Colonel Bonneville this dread news, but found that the commanding officer had left that morning by train for Washington to receive his final orders. Acting in his impetuous way, Tripler wrote a letter directly to the Surgeon General expressing the opinion it would be "murder" for the regiment to attempt an Isthmus crossing while the epidemic was in progress. Tripler recommended postponing the move until the end of the rainy season, or shipping the regiment around Cape Horn. When the letter arrived in Washington, the Surgeon General showed it to Bonneville. Bonneville became enraged at his subordinate for writing the letter, and refused to consider delaying departure or making the long voyage around Cape Horn. He told the Surgeon General he would lead his troops across the Isthmus "too rapidly for the epidemic to catch them." The Surgeon General acquiesced and did not intercede. Tripler's letter acted only to increase the commander's dislike for him. On his return from Washington Bonneville told his adjutant that they must be on guard against "acts of future treachery on the part of the surgeon and the quartermaster."

The War Department had booked passage for the regiment—troops, dependents and baggage—on the U. S. Mail Steam Line ship *Ohio,* one of the largest steamers afloat. In addition to the sea passage to Panama the contract also called for transit across the Isthmus and steamer transportation from Panama City to San Francisco. Steamer tickets still sold at a premium in 1852 and even the large companies engaged in shady practices, reserving more tickets than a ship's space allowed and then canceling some of the reservations at the last minute. When Lieutenant Grant, as part of his duties as quartermaster, personally contacted the ticket agent of the U. S. Mail Steam Line in New York, he found that all of the 250 first-class cabins and 80 of the steerage bunks on the *Ohio* had already been sold to civilians, leaving space for only 550 regimental troops and dependents.

When Grant informed Colonel Bonneville that the *Ohio* was 150 bunks short of the regiment's requirements, the commander responded with what Eunice Tripler described as "the most uncouth tantrum I have ever seen a grown man, much less an officer of the military service of any nation, engage in. He seemed to hold Lieutenant Grant solely responsible for acts which had been made in Washington."

Grant accepted the tongue-lashing stoically, although, indeed, he had not been connected in any way with making the passage contract, and then hurried about seeking additional space. He found a steamer bound for California around Cape Horn which agreed to squeeze in two companies of the regiment. The men of these two companies grumbled as they hastily assembled their gear and boarded the ship. Their voyage would take them weeks longer than the others, but later events proved their longer voyage to be a blessing. Grant then supervised the building of tiers of temporary bunks on the decks of the *Ohio*. On July 7 the remaining eight companies, the band, headquarters detachment and the dependents—550 in all—crowded aboard. Next day the *Ohio* dropped downriver past Sandy Hook, its paddle wheels churning foam from the placid sea, and turned south. Counting troops, civilians and crew there were over 1,100 passengers on the crowded ship.

The health of the regiment was generally good on the voyage to Panama. The bandmaster was stricken with severe diarrhea which did not respond to treatment, but his was the only serious illness. On rough days the flying-serpent prow of the *Ohio* rose and fell in an increasing arc, the ship riding higher and higher in the water as she used up her coal. Grant and others suffered from seasickness, but most of the regiment enjoyed the voyage.

The *Ohio* dropped anchor in Navy Bay off Aspinwall on July 16 after an eight-day voyage. The civilian passengers went ashore first in the yawls and then the military disembarked. In his memoirs Grant recalled this was a day of "torrential showers alternating with hot sun." Despite the amount of work that the railroad company had done in building up Manzanillo, Grant reported most of the island area "covered with eight to ten inches of water." The frame buildings on stilts stood about in the lagoon-like interior of the island, connected by flimsy wooden footwalks. Grant said, "I could not understand how any person could live many months in Aspinwall and . . . still more why anyone tried." He commented upon "the stench of the slops," and the "slab hotels, boarding houses and bordellos."

The miserable town was a discouraging sight, indeed, to the regimental quartermaster, coping with rain-soaked women and children, ammunition chests, tents, band instruments, mess kettles and the other odds and ends of regimental property. Under the treaty with Colombia, members of foreign armies could not carry their firearms on the Isthmus. So, heavy cases of rifles and pistols were added to the quartermaster stores. Most of the officers and noncommissioned officers retained their swords. Ostensibly these were "accouterments for ceremonial purposes," but they came in handy in chopping through the jungle and disciplining recalcitrant natives.

After landing, the troops were delayed again while the civilians were sent forward first on the train. Grant drafted most of the men to help load baggage and gear on boxcars, but others slipped away to see the sights. Tripler had lectured them on the perils of drinking liquor and eating the local fruit, but many soldiers ignored the warning and drank great quantities of liquor. Some returned to the docks carrying stalks of ripe bananas which the women and children seized upon eagerly. Try as he might, Tripler could not prevent them from eating the fruit and drinking water sold by the water carriers.

Before leaving the ship, the surgeon examined the stricken bandmaster and decided that he was too ill to be moved ashore. The bandmaster died two days later, the only military casualty on the voyage from New York to Aspinwall.

While the regiment waited for the train, Dr. Tripler had an opportunity to visit the railroad hospital and speak with the doctors there. He received grim news. Cholera had caused so many deaths that railroad construction work had ceased. The able-bodied employees remaining on duty were occupied full time in maintaining the tracks and running the trains. Forty workers out of 100 assigned at one station had died. An entire shipload of Irish laborers from Cork, arriving a few weeks before, had caught the disease within a week and most of them had died. Tripler learned with foreboding that the disease was widespread; epidemics were in progress at both Cruces and Gorgona, towns through which the regiment had to pass.

George Totten advised Colonel Bonneville and his quartermaster that he had only two locomotives available and each was too light to pull a train carrying the entire regiment at once. Therefore, he would have to divide the military group into two trains which would leave Aspinwall about an hour apart. The boxcars loaded with regimental equipment would remain behind to be picked up by one of the returning locomotives. At that time the railroad tracks extended about 22 miles from Manzanillo, stopping abruptly in the jungle a mile short of the village of Barbacoas on the Chagres. The last mile of right of way had been cleared and leveled, said Totten, and passengers could easily walk that distance. But Totten agreed to loan Grant mule carts to carry his heavy baggage from the end of the track to the river dock.

Colonel Bonneville announced that he would take most of the able-bodied troops on the first train. On arrival at Barbacoas he would lead his group upriver at once to Gorgona and march overland from there to Panama City. The remainder—consisting of the sick, the women, children, baggage and one company for guards—would follow in the second train and go in boats upriver past Gorgona to Cruces. From Cruces this group would ride muleback to Panama City. The Cruces road was known to be rough, but was shorter than the Gorgona road by two miles. According to the travel agreement signed in New York, a contractor would have mules ready and waiting at Cruces.

Prior to his leaving, Bonneville warned the surgeon and the quartermaster to guard against "acts of treachery." Eunice Tripler said that the commander did not make it clear whether he expected "treachery" to issue from the Isthmus natives or from her husband and Lieutenant Grant. Bonneville gave the two a direct warning that if any harm came to the dependents as a result of their laxity or dereliction of duty, he would see them court-martialed and cashiered from the service. With that final pronouncement, the crochety commander boarded the train and departed.

The second group followed several hours later. On arrival at the end of the tracks they loaded the baggage into the mule carts and then marched along the cleared right of way to Barbacoas. Grant offered to let the ladies and children ride in the carts, but most declined. Led by Mrs. Tripler, who carried a bright parasol, they strolled behind the slow-moving carts. It was a relief to stretch one's legs after nine days of crowded ship and train. Occasional rain showers sprinkled them, but did not dampen their spirits. The countryside—"fine fields of Indian corn dotted with heavy green islands of palm groves"—was pleasant to look upon. "Our way was lightened by occasional bursts of song from the ladies of the group," wrote Delia Sheffield. "Dr. Tripler, who had a fine tenor voice, would join in on the choruses. Then he would slyly suggest that Lieutenant Grant sing a solo for us, but that gentleman would only smile in his usual way and say nothing."

On arrival at Barbacoas Grant rented all available craft and started sending his group upstream at once. There were only enough boats to send half the party that afternoon, so he put the first group in charge of a subaltern and Sergeant Sheffield and sent them ahead. Grant described the boats as being large—"able to hold thirty to forty passengers." He said they had planks running along the sides and that the boatmen standing on these planks would "start from the bow, place one end of his pole against the river bottom, brace his shoulders and walk to the stern as rapidly as possible." He estimated their speed upstream at from a mile to a mile and a half an hour. The native polers, he said, "were not seriously encumbered with clothing."

The near-naked boatmen frightened the women and children of the party with their wild looks and sudden outbursts of "heathenish song," and Grant watched with foreboding each load disappear upstream "in the care of such savages." As he was about to take a well-earned rest, word came back by a native messenger that one boatload of the women and children had capsized and all were drowned. Grant and Lieutenant Henry Wallen, whose wife and two small children had been sent ahead in the boats, rushed upstream. Wallen said later, "We had not proceeded far, however, before we ascertained that the boat which had turned over contained a number of civilian passengers, and . . . that none of our party was injured."

That night the first group tied up on the river bank near a village where a wedding celebration was in progress. All the boatmen departed to drink the native rum and join the festivities. Delia Sheffield wrote, "All that night the women and children shivered in the boats as the boatmen howled like drunken barbarians in the village." The few soldiers accompanying the party fingered their swords and cursed the lack of firearms. Finally the long night was over. The boatmen reappeared, sullen and disheveled, and began poling again. Daylight brought the passengers fresh courage.

The boxcars loaded with regimental equipment did not appear at the end of the track until after dark on July 17. On searching the cars early next morning, Dr. Tripler was dismayed to find that none of his medical supplies were on the cars. He dispatched a sergeant to Aspinwall on the unloaded train to search for the missing items, then helped Grant load the last group of dependents and baggage into the boats for Cruces. These pushed off before 8 a.m. Grant found boats for the remaining equipment, and then he departed, leaving Tripler to await his medical supplies. Late that afternoon the sergeant returned in a handcar almost empty-handed, bearing "only four packages out of thirty," in Tripler's words. The sergeant had rum on his breath and staggered when he walked. Tripler immediately suspected he had spent more time in the cantinas on Manzanillo than in searching for the missing supplies. After giving the sergeant a severe tongue-lashing and threatening to prosecute him for dereliction of duty, the surgeon appropriated the handcar and rode back to Manzanillo himself that evening.

Tripler found his missing 26 packages of medical supplies in the first boxcar he searched next morning, confirming his suspicion that the sergeant had not been diligent. George Totten ordered the boxcar attached to a locomotive and sent it and the doctor roaring back to Barbacoas at top speed. At the end of the track, with the help of a railroad section foreman, Tripler hired two scrawny mules to pack his supplies the last mile to the river dock. There, after more delay spent haggling, he hired a large bungo for the trip to Cruces, arriving there at 9:30 p.m., Monday, July 19.

Lieutenant Grant had arrived at Cruces on the morning of Sunday, July 18. While his men unloaded the boats, Grant hurried away to see the contractor about the promised mules. He was disappointed to find no animals immediately available, but the contractor assured Grant he would have them next day. Grant, returning to his group, gave orders to pitch tents and prepare to stay overnight. Since it was Sunday, Mrs. Tripler requested that Lieutenant Grant, as senior officer, "hold some form of Christian service, or at least read us a passage from the Holy Scripture and say a few words which will lift up our hearts." Grant agreed and the ladies, the children and some of the troops sat on the grass while Grant stood on a small packing case and thumbed through Mrs. Tripler's Bible, seeking an appropriate passage. Cognizant of the mounting homesickness of his party, he read them from the 127th Psalm: "By the rivers of Babylon, there we sat down, yea, we wept, when we remembered Zion."

"It was an inspiring experience in that heathenish land," wrote Mrs. Tripler, "to hear the word of God read by a uniformed member of our American military service. Then when Lieutenant Grant spoke us a few words of comfort, taking for his message, 'How shall we sing the Lord's song in a strange land?', most of our women wept openly and I noticed several of our doughty bearded veterans, enured to hardship though they were, drying their eyes."

Looking back, one can see that it was really not so remarkable that the phlegmatic Grant could deliver a moving speech when he desired. He had engaged in debating with some success at West Point, and while a member of a temperance group at Sackett's Harbor had frequently led public discussions on the evils of drink. His reputation for mediocrity which comes down to us seems to stem mainly from the unprepossessing visage we see in paintings and photographs. He was certainly not imposing in appearance, but during periods of trial in his Army career he always found the ability to rise to whatever height the occasion demanded. Thus, on the banks of the Chagres River, while inwardly fretting over the lack of mules and the dangers of disease, he managed to divert the thoughts of his charges from their fears, with the ancient tale of the children of Israel.

That night there was group singing and a spelling bee for the youngsters. "We Christian women did not forget the education of our children, even in the jungle," said Delia Sheffield. Mrs. Sheffield at the time she made the Panama crossing was only fifteen, but highly impressed by her recently won status as a married woman. "We noted that Lieutenant Grant, who habitually had a cheery word for the women and children, was silent. My husband told me, in the privacy of our tent, that the lieutenant was worried about mules."

The worry was not unfounded. Next day the contractor still had no pack animals and his promises were beginning to sound thin. When Dr. Tripler arrived at Cruces that evening, he found the group "camped out in tents with the baggage and regimental gear stacked in a neat pile." Grant reported that all of the sick had recovered and that the contractor had promised mules the next morning.

Next morning, Tuesday, July 20, the contractor still had no mules. Tripler decided to utilize the delay by disciplining the sergeant who had failed to find the medical supplies. The surgeon sent his orderly to summon the man. The orderly returned very soon with the report that the sergeant was ill in his tent. Certain that he would find the man intoxicated and liable for additional charges, Tripler went to see for himself. The sight and smell inside the tent froze Tripler's anger into apprehension. The sergeant was lying in a tightly jackknifed position holding his stomach, retching and defecating uncontrollably. His pulse was weak and his staring eyes had sunk deep in the sockets. Tripler immediately quarantined the tent and hastened to tell Grant that there was a case of "malignant cholera" in the camp. The sergeant died six hours later.

"I was sure now," wrote Grant, "that the scarcity of pack animals was such that we were never going to get them in the foreseeable future at the rates called for in the contract." The agreement made in New York called for the Army to pay $16 a mule for a person to ride from Cruces to Panama City and a baggage rate of 11 cents a pound. Making a contract at these prices was an act of either criminal ignorance or out-and-out perfidy on the part of the U. S. Mail Steam Line agent. Everyone doing business on the Isthmus at that time, Grant said bitterly in his memoirs, "knew that muleteers at Cruces and Gorgona were demanding from $20 to $40 a mule for riders and charging a baggage rate of 16 to 20 cents a pound." To make matters worse, the Army had been preceded to Cruces by a large number of the civilian passengers from the *Ohio*. Said Tripler: "We had the vexation of seeing hundreds of citizens forwarded without detention while we waited five days." Grant commented to Tripler that he had seen some civilians pay as much as $40 to ride the 25 miles to Panama City "on a mule that would not bring ten dollars on any market in the United States." But the grim fact was that mules of any sort were scarce. During some weeks in the 1850's as many as 4,000 travelers crossed the Isthmus each way, frantic to get to the gold diggings or just as frantic to get home, and they would pay exorbitant prices.

Next morning, on learning that a child had died in one of the tents during the night and that several more cases of cholera had appeared, Grant began hiring mules at any price, and sending his charges in a frantic exodus from Cruces.

Tripler wrote: "The moment a rider or a cargo is placed upon a mule's back that moment he must set out, or the muleteer will strip his mule and carry him off." Once in the saddle, each soldier, woman or child, sick or well, was on his own. The march from Cruces to Panama City was "a straggling one," Tripler said with great understatement.

In paying the high prices, Grant soon ran out of regimental funds and had to order those remaining to walk to Panama City. The regimental drum major said that his wife was too weak to walk the distance. Grant handed the man $25 from his own pocket and told him to try and rent a mule from some private individual. The drum major was unsuccessful in finding one. Then Grant told him and his wife to keep the money and wait in Cruces in the hope an animal would turn up. The wife said she would rather die on the trail than risk waiting longer in the village, and asked Grant for a pair of Army pantaloons to wear on the hike. He immediately gave her a pair. The wife made the long walk without a mishap, but her "unladylike appearance" on arrival at Panama City later became a source of embarrassment to Grant.

The trek was one of terrible hardship; only after the passage of years would anyone recall the affair with any humor. Little Mrs. Sheffield was one of the first women fortunate enough to obtain a mule. Led by a native guide, "an almost completely unclothed savage," she rode along the trail a few rods ahead of a group of walkers under command of her husband. As darkness fell, the native guide suddenly tried to lead both mule and rider into a hut nearby. Convinced that the guide had "carnal designs" on her person, Mrs. Sheffield began screaming and beating both mule and native with a heavy cane which she carried for protection. This assault caused the mule "to rear and pitch in the most disconcerting way possible," and her screams brought Sergeant Sheffield and several soldiers running, brandishing their swords. While the men secured and quieted the mule, the native was allowed to escape into the jungle. "I felt at the time that my rescuers were more concerned about the welfare of the dumb brute than they were with the preservation of my honor," said Mrs. Sheffield.

Grant's friends the Wallens had a bad scare. Lieutenant Wallen's seven-year-old son rode a porter's back and his four-year-old daughter, Nannie, a hammock slung between two porters. The second night on the trail Nannie and her bearers did not reach the camp. Mrs. Wallen cried hysterically throughout the night while her husband paced restlessly about the campfire, awaiting dawn. Next morning the bearers brought Nannie Wallen in safe and sound, sucking on piece of sugar cane. They had spent the night at their home, a hut in the jungle just a few hundred yards from the Army camp.

After Grant had sent on most of his group, he found six Sisters of Charity in one of the Cruces huts. They had been among the civilian passengers from the *Ohio*. When one of them became ill in Cruces, the others delayed their journey to nurse her. Grant again "exceeded his authority" by hiring native bearers to carry the nuns to Panama City slung in hammocks.

During the last two frantic days at Cruces more cases of cholera appeared and four more people died. One man who successfully survived his bout with the disease had to be left in care of the alcalde because he was too weak to travel. After burying the last of the dead, Grant followed with the rear guard to Panama City.

Some of the walkers, suddenly stricken, fell out on the trail. Dr. Tripler did what he could for them. Three died. One fell into a sinkhole and his body disappeared before the surgeon could get to him. The native guides and muleteers were indifferent to their troubles. Quarreling seemed the only activity which roused them from their lethargy. Once, when two groups of guides flashed knives, the Army men stepped in and restored order. "My husband beat one of the Indians about the head and shoulders so smartly with the flat side of his sword that the man screamed with pain and tried to escape," reported Mrs. Sheffield. "But two of our men held him while my husband gave him a further taste of the flat steel and soon all the Indians resumed their interest in leading the mules."

Dr. Tripler arrived in Panama City after dark on July 22. He learned that Bonneville's group had passed three nights on the trail from Gorgona and had suffered several deaths from cholera. Bonneville had taken his group at once to the steamer *Golden Gate* anchored off Taboga, 12 miles down the bay, despite the fact that cholera had broken out on the ship, and had left orders that as soon as other groups straggled in, they too were to come to the steamer.

The *Golden Gate* could be contacted only once a day, by a steam launch that left the dock at Panama City at 5 p.m. Since he had arrived too late for the launch, Dr. Tripler had to wait until next day to report to his commander. At the temporary hospital set up at the U. S. Consul's office, Tripler learned that the civilian group from the *Ohio* which had so seriously depleted the mule supply at Cruces had not been spared. Six of them had died of cholera after arrival at Panama City.

Grant, pushing rather than leading the final group of groaning, mud-spattered, vomiting soldiers and civilians, arrived early on the afternoon of July 23. He estimated that "about one-third of the people" he had brought from the end of the tracks at Barbacoas "had died, either at Cruces or on the way to Panama." He accompanied Tripler to the *Golden Gate* on the steam launch. They found the high-hatted commander in a near-hysterical state. Conditions aboard the ship were bad enough to frighten even the most courageous, and Bonneville had made matters worse by mixing the sick and well indiscriminately in the military quarters. Delia Sheffield, sent aboard with the others, reported seeing "strong men walking the deck suddenly begin writhing with cramps and be carried off to die."

Many of the enlisted men, fearful of contracting the disease, deserted, swimming from the ship to Taboga and hiring bungos to the mainland. Bonneville, screaming with rage, had them pursued, apprehended and brought back to the ship in irons. So, in addition to the groans of the dying, the spectators were entertained by the screams of soldiers being flogged as punishment for attempted desertion.

The arrival of Tripler and Grant gave the commander two new scapegoats. He held Grant responsible for "the shocking unladylike appearance of the drum major's wife." That female had arrived on the *Golden Gate* wearing the pantaloons that Grant had issued her for the hike from Cruces. When her husband told Bonneville of the circumstances, the commander threatened to have both the drum major and Grant court-martialed for "gross misuse of Government property." Others had told him that Lieutenant Grant had spent all of the regimental funds by paying more for mules than the authorized $16 rate. This was "misappropriation of Government funds," Bonneville said darkly, and matters would go much harder for Grant "than they had in Mexico."

Then the commander loudly denounced both Tripler and

Grant in front of the passengers of the *Golden Gate,* blaming all of the regiment's troubles on their "treachery." Grant remained silent under the abuse, but Tripler told the commander that he would report Bonneville's "criminal actions" regarding the mixing of sick and well to the Surgeon General. Ignoring Bonneville's order to remain on the *Golden Gate* and tend the sick there, Tripler went back to Panama City in the launch and arranged to lease an old hulk anchored in the harbor to serve as a hospital ship. Returning to the *Golden Gate* and continuing to ignore the commander's protests, the doctor had all the sick soldiers and dependents removed for quarantine on the hulk. There Dr. Tripler took charge of nursing the sick, vainly fighting a disease which he did not understand. "The usual means were tried with the usual want of success. Free exhibition of brandy with capiscum and chloride sodium was about as successful as anything," Tripler reported later to the Surgeon General. "I found that acetas plumbi, in doses of five to ten grains, valuable in restraining the diarrhea." Then he mentioned experimenting with doses of calomel, camphor and quinine, and such external treatment as mustard plasters, hot water bottles and massage.

Even on the hospital ship, Dr. Tripler was not free from the attention of Colonel Bonneville. The commander appeared daily in a rowboat from the *Golden Gate.* Remaining at a safe distance from the hulk, Bonneville called out orders to the surgeon, demanding all sorts of nonsensical procedures and reports. His patience exhausted, Tripler screamed unprintable oaths at his tormentor. These heated exchanges were plainly audible to the passengers on the *Golden Gate.*

Eunice Tripler wrote, "I am sure that the Almighty in His infinite mercy took note of the overwhelming nature of the terrible trials He had seen fit to shower on the heads of my poor husband and his lunatic of a commander; otherwise, He would have sent a bolt of lightning to destroy them both for the blasphemies which they shouted at each other." Mrs. Tripler, who remained on the *Golden Gate* with the other wives while her husband tended his patients on the hulk, said that on one occasion Colonel Bonneville, "greatly exercised," returned from one of his towboat altercations with the surgeon and had "the ungentlemanly audacity to say that Surgeon Tripler had displayed a traitorous excess of authority and that his days in the service were numbered." Mrs. Tripler lost no time in sending a messenger to inform her husband what Bonneville had said. The surgeon came at once to confront the Mad Hatter on the bridge of the *Golden Gate*. "My husband was bristling with rage," reported Mrs. Tripler. Hatless, with his long hair and side-whiskers in wild disarray, the surgeon had the appearance of an angry prophet from the Old Testament. According to one officer who observed the altercation, Tripler towered over Bonneville and called him "A g-d d----d scoundrel and nitwit, and a g-d d----d butcher and hellhound as well."

The religious Mrs. Tripler, who had long quivered with apprehension at the thought of divine retribution for her husband's blasphemous language, was present at the confrontation, but reported only that her husband told Bonneville "to go ahead and make his threats good." In any case, Bonneville never brought any charges against either Tripler or Grant for their conduct on the Isthmus, although for years afterward the War Department harassed Grant by trying to collect his "excessive expenditures incurred during the crossing," and Grant always felt Bonneville was behind it.

The epidemic continued to run its course with burials occurring several times a day. The passengers aboard the *Golden Gate* would hear the sound of the bugle blowing "taps" and run to the rail. They watched figures on the hulk, small in the distance, roll a burlap-wrapped body with a cannon ball at the toe into the bay. Then they waited fearfully to hear the name of the one buried, to learn if it was a friend or loved one. One evening a request came from the hulk for another bugler. The man who had blown taps at two funerals that morning had just died of the disease and there was no one on the hulk to sound the horn for him.

The cholera patients were transferred from the *Golden Gate* to the hulk on Saturday, July 24. By the following Tuesday Tripler noted that the epidemic seemed to be abating; there were no new cases. He was also heartened by a rising percentage of recoveries, and wrote in his journal: "The chances are that the cases first attacked will die and that the ratio of the mortality will diminish with the duration of the epidemic."

Then an event occurred which Tripler blamed for another outbreak of the disease. "When the steamer (steam launch) came that day it brought a dozen knapsacks which had been moulding. The owners claimed them eagerly and changed their clothing. Many fell sick in performing this act. Twenty hours later all were ill with cholera and most died." Here Tripler added still another myth to the cholera theory of the 1850's—contagion from mouldy clothing.

During his time on the hulk Tripler was hampered by lack of help. Enlisted men had to be ordered aboard for nurse duty and virtually kept prisoner. Grant was the only other officer ordered by Bonneville to stay aboard the hospital ship. As quartermaster, Grant methodically went about the business of furnishing burlap sacking and cannon balls for the burials of the dead. Tripler suggested that some of the other regimental officers "volunteer for duty on the hulk, as a means of inspiring and encouraging the disheartened and frightened men." Captain John Gore was among those volunteering to come, doing so over the tearful protests of his wife. Gore, Grant's comrade from the Mexican War, was a seasoned veteran whose presence on the hulk helped quiet some of the fears of those held aboard against their will.

On July 29 Tripler made arrangements to have those convalescing put ashore in huts and tents on the island of Flamenco, in the Bay of Panama, six miles offshore. After helping in the transfer of the patients, Captain Gore returned to the *Golden Gate*. On August 1, while indulging in a game of euchre with his wife, Mrs. Tripler and a subaltern, Gore dropped his cards suddenly and said, "I think I've caught it."

"The major [Gore held the brevet rank of major] was suddenly very pale," said Mrs. Tripler. She summoned her husband from Flamenco. Gore died that night. His was the last cholera death. He was the only commissioned officer of the regiment to succumb to the disease. To Grant fell the melancholy task of sending Mrs. Gore and her infant son home to Kentucky. Escorted by Lieutenant McFeeley, the youngest officer of the regiment, she set off to retrace the terrible journey across the Isthmus back to Aspinwall. Mrs. Gore rode in one hammock slung between natives, her child's nurse in another, and her young son rode the shoulders of a native carrier. When Lieutenant McFeeley returned to the regiment on the West Coast five months later, he reported that the native carriers had stolen all of Mrs. Gore's silver and jewelry and most of her extra clothing.

Bonneville took up the officer's death as another issue against Tripler and Grant. He had hardly been friendly with Gore while he was alive, but now the commander made a martyr of him, putting the blame for his death on the hapless surgeon and quartermaster. "The idiocies of the commander are endless," Tripler said to his wife. Grant, as usual, kept silent. Even in his memoirs, he made no complaint against Bonneville.

Bonneville now informed his command that the sailing of the *Golden Gate* was imminent. Tripler recommended that before sailing all knapsacks aboard should be destroyed and the ship fumigated with chlorine. The *Golden Gate* was a new vessel, commissioned in 1851, one of the most luxurious ships afloat at that time. The captain refused to consider Tripler's recommendation, so the surgeon took the matter to Consul Nelson. Nelson appeared on board and told the captain that if he sailed without fumigating, he would be denied harbor privileges on his return. The captain grudgingly submitted. Luckily, there were no casualties from the deadly fumes. Tripler reported that the rats left the steamer, "dropping in great squealing, squeaking swarms into the bay." Thus one primary source of infection was eliminated.

There was one humorous incident arising out of the fumigation procedure. All of the passengers from the *Golden Gate*, including the uniformed military personnel aboard, were moved on rafts from the ship to Flamenco Island while the ship was being processed. As the rafts, loaded with people and equipment, were being towed ashore, the lone New Granadan warship, an armed tug, came steaming out from Panama City, ready for war. Alert shore authorities, noticing the movement through spyglasses, had leaped to the conclusion that a filibuster attack on the city was about to be launched. The tug commander was finally convinced that the movement was a peaceable one.

On August 3 the captain of the *Golden Gate* announced that he would sail the next day. Still rankled that Tripler had caused his ship to be fumigated, the captain said he would take only 450 members of the regiment. He said also that he would not transport any of the civilian dependents at Army rates and not a single sick man from Flamenco could be brought aboard. Dr. Tripler shook his fist in the captain's face and told him it was a breach of contract and a fraud, and that the captain had no authority to limit the number of military passengers in any fashion. To Tripler's disgust, Colonel Bonneville bowed to the will of the captain. Bonneville, fed up with the Isthmus and ready to leave at the cost of any concession, could not resist a final thrust at his hated surgeon. He ordered Tripler to remain on Flamenco with those still sick, and make arrangements to come on a later ship, as best he could. Tripler contracted with a Dr. Deal of California, a civilian physician aboard the *Golden Gate,* to look after the medical needs of the troops on the voyage to California. Then the *Golden Gate* steamed away on August 4. The 4th Infantry Regiment had lost 80 men to cholera on the Isthmus plus an unrecorded number of women and children.

Tripler nursed his sick back to health on Flamenco, and canvassed all arriving ships for space to California. He was treated like a leper. No one wanted his group. Most ship captains would not even let him come aboard, for fear he would bring contagion. Finally, after several days of begging and cajoling, the captain of the *Northerner,* supported by a round-robin vote of his passengers, agreed to take the group as a "patriotic gesture."

That generous move almost ended in disaster. The *Northerner* sent a leaky scow to pick up the passengers from Flamenco and it foundered, but luckily the water was shallow. Some baggage was lost and the passengers received a wetting. Then, some of the civilian passengers on the *Northerner* objected to stretcher cases being brought aboard. They thought these were still "infectious." Tripler finally had to leave half a dozen of his patients behind in the care of the U. S. Consul. The doctor sailed at last on August 8, after spending four of the most frightful weeks of his life in managing the passage across the Isthmus.

In a letter of August 9, 1852, written aboard the *Golden Gate*, "Near Acapulco," Grant told his wife some of the details of the trip but spared her the more harrowing ones. "Although we have had terrible sickness among the troops, and have lost one hundred persons, counting men, women & children, yet I have enjoyed good health. It has been the province of my place as Quarter Master to be exposed to the weather and the climate on the Isthmus while most of the others were quietly aboard ship, but to that very activity probably may be ascribed my good health." He mentioned nothing concerning his difficulties with Bonneville and spoke only of the future when his darling Julia and children could join him at his new garrison post.

On August 31, after observing the survivors of the 4th Regiment at Benicia Barracks, California, Major Osborne Cross wrote the Quartermaster General in Washington that the regimental "loss has been seriously great, while those who have arrived are broken down with diseases, the seeds of which were engendered on the Isthmus." Major Cross suggested all troops in the future be sent around Cape Horn.

As long as Grant lived he would talk more of the hellish march across Panama than of any of his famous battles. The rain, the mud, the sick and the dying on the jungle trail made a lifelong impression on him. In his old age he told his intimates that the burdens put on him by the incompetent Bonneville had served at least one good purpose by revealing to him his own "unguessed powers at this business of managing a command of military men."

The Rubicon Is Passed!

DURING THE TERRIBLE SUMMER OF 1852 MANY OF THE RAILROAD workers who toppled over in the jungle managed to drag themselves to the tracks, where they were picked up and taken to the hospital in Aspinwall. Others, swallowed by the sinkholes or eaten alive by ants and land crabs, disappeared without a trace. Fifty-one engineers, surveyors and draftsmen—Totten's entire technical staff with the exception of James Baldwin—died in the epidemic.

By late August the disease had run its course, disappearing as mysteriously as it had come. The weakened survivors, moving about in a dazed, disorganized fashion, found it hard to get started again. But the directors in New York would tolerate no further delay. There was too much money at stake. Construction must begin again, immediately. The directors sent Totten a new technical staff, and orders to get the tracks moving.

Importing 1,000 African Negroes with whip-carrying Arab overseers, Totten pushed the rails beyond Barbacoas across a level region of meadows where the land had been cultivated since

Spanish times. But the road was still breached by the river at Barbacoas, and a serious dispute arose over the type of bridge to be built there, a dispute between Totten and the board of directors, delaying construction.

The Chagres at Barbacoas was 300 feet wide, flowing in a deep rocky channel. In the dry season the river was a lazy trickle, but the advent of the rains brought sudden, restless freshets which could raise the water level as much as 40 feet in a single night. Totten wanted to build an iron bridge, a heavy structure which would withstand the decaying forces of the tropical climate as well as the torrential onslaughts of the wet season. The directors wanted a wooden-trestle bridge—hastily constructed. Timber was cheaper than iron and faster to work with. Speed was the director's main concern. They wanted the railroad completed to Panama City as soon as possible. Heated, acrimonious letters passed back and forth.

During October of 1852, while Totten wrote long, detailed letters in his neat engineer's handwriting, trying to convince the management that an iron bridge was a necessity at Barbacoas, John L. Stephens died in New York of fever contracted on the Isthmus. His death was a great loss to the Panama Railroad Company, and in particular to Totten. Of all the directors, Stephens was the only one who knew the Isthmus intimately. Had he lived, he would no doubt have upheld the construction superintendent's stand for an iron bridge. But Stephens was dead and Totten was left to fight his battle alone. William C. Young, appointed president of the company, knew nothing of the tropics and showed no desire to learn of them by coming to the Isthmus. The issue over the bridge became a bitter personal quarrel between Totten and Young.

While the quarrel delayed railroad progress, the fortunes of Runnels Express Service continued to flourish. Runnels spent most of his time on the Pacific side of the Isthmus, but his men continued their surveillance of ships arriving at Manzanillo, ever on the alert for leopards and tigers who were hiding their spots and stripes. His mass hanging of the 37 evil-doers on the sea wall at Panama City in the spring of 1852 had, it seemed, paralyzed the activities of the Derienni. The summer had brought the cholera epidemic, a democratic affliction wreaking its toll on the criminal and law-abiding population equally. Many travelers died on the Isthmus trails that summer, but not because of the Derienni. The pack trains, guarded only by scanty crews, made the crossing without armed interference and even single travelers could walk the entire way unscathed, if they successfully eluded the cholera.

Then, slowly and insidiously, with the return of the healthier dry season, banditry and murder began again. At first only the single traveler or the pack train straggler on lonely stretches of the trail had to be wary, but then the armed attacks became more daring and overt. Gunfire flashed from the jungle thickets and masked riders harassed the main bodies of the pack trains. Even the towns were not safe. During the fall of 1852 a group of bandits stormed into a crowded barroom in Gorgona, robbed the gambling tables, and withdrew under a covering fusillade of shots which left four patrons sprawled dead on the floor.

Henry Tracy, the Wells Fargo agent in Panama City, a gloomy oracle in criminal matters, wrote to his home office, "It seems that more bloodshed and funerals is in the offing for your humble obedient servant on the Isthmus. Please send me by urgent express four (4) additional buck shot guns, with ample powder and ball for same."

In October of 1852 John McGlynn, a paymaster for the Panama Railroad Company, was attacked as he walked along the tracks near Bohío Soldado and robbed of a section gang payroll amounting to $300. Wounded seriously, McGlynn was left to die, but before expiring he revealed the identity of his assailant, a recent arrival on the Strip from Cincinnati named Timothy Copeland. This attack on a railroad employee on company property called for immediate action. After a conference in the chambers of Consul Nelson, Runnels was dispatched to apprehend and punish Copeland, "In a manner," said Nelson, "calculated to be the most immediate, effective and exemplary that you can devise to insure that this flagrant attack on a railroad employee not be repeated."

On his arrival in Aspinwall, Runnels learned more information derogatory to Copeland's character and conduct. Just after the robbery of McGlynn Copeland had appeared at the *Maison del Vieux Carre,* a house of prostitution. The *Maison,* which specialized in French girls, was the most expensive house in Aspinwall. Copeland had displayed a large roll of currency and offered to pay a young prostitute $50 for her company that evening. The girl accepted the money and led him upstairs to her chamber. Next morning she was found strangled in her bed. The $50 was gone, as well as her savings and some jewelry from under the mattress. No one had seen the girl or Copeland come downstairs again after they had gone up together. The window of the room was open, and foot tracks below showed that someone had dropped to the ground. Copeland, described as "a tall man with a white, cadaverous countenance and pale eyes staring from under the brim of a misshapen black hat," had not left town. He was still swaggering around the streets and drinking in the saloons. He claimed to have ridden with the highwayman Murrell on the Natchez Trace and openly bragged of the number of men he had killed. On hearing that there was some talk of lynching him for the murder of the girl, Copeland had reacted by brandishing an evil-looking dirk and challenging anyone to try. This brought much applause and adulation in the Bottle Alley saloons where such as he had many admirers.

Runnels and two members of his Isthmus Guard found Copeland in one of these same saloons. The three were carrying blunt, double-barreled buckshot guns. Most of the patrons scrambled for exits. The buckshot guns, the size of small cannons, could sweep the room clean of practically everybody.

Copeland is supposed to have asked with drunken bravado, "What are you going to do with me?"

Runnels, after taking Copeland's pistol and dirk, told him that he must accompany them to the *Maison.* Copeland protested, but Runnels was adamant. With his arms bound, Copeland was marched to the house of prostitution where he was identified as the man who had gone upstairs with the murdered girl. Some jewelry found in Copeland's pockets—a diamond ring and "an ormolu bracelet set with small green stones"—was identified as having been the property of the girl.

Copeland, still wearing the cloak of bravado, again asked Runnels, "in a tone both bold and insolent," according to the newspaper account, what Runnels was going to do with him.

Runnels answered, "I'm going to hang you."

Copeland then broke down and begged for his life, saying that he had come from a good home in Cincinnati and asked for mercy in the name of his elderly parents.

"He had decided that to be a living dog was better than a dead lion," Runnels wrote, according to his sister. "But his crimes were too grievous for him to be allowed mercy."

Copeland was marched by his captors from the *Maison* to the railroad area behind the long shed-like wharf. They were followed by a growing crowd. Runnels fashioned a hangman's knot and looped it about Copeland's neck. He attached the other end to a derrick-like hoist operated by a steam engine, which was used to raise heavy pieces of equipment.

Copeland fell to his knees and begged the crowd to prevent Runnels from taking his life. The onlookers responded with jeers and catcalls.

The Reverend Isaiah Cranston of Providence, Rhode Island, who had arrived in Aspinwall that very day on the schooner *Mary Ellen,* stepped forward to intercede. "Captain Runnels then told me what the man had done," reported Cranston in his journal. "Captain Runnels displayed a small canvas bag which had been in Paymaster McGlynn's possession when he was shot, and some pieces of jewelry, formerly the property of the murdered harlot. These, Captain Runnels said, he had found in the pockets of Timothy Copeland. I knew from this evidence that the wretched prisoner was guilty and that it was useless to plead for mercy for him."

After his conversation with Cranston, Runnels grasped the lever which operated the steam engine.

"I have stood upon Gallows Hill and have seen my share of

the spectacles there," wrote Reverend Cranston. "I can truthfully say that I have never seen an execution conducted in such a bizarre and extended manner. The man, Copeland, hoisted slowly into the air, was in truth strangled to death by a puffing steam engine! Such is the progress of man that machinery can now be made to perform this grim but necessary work. They had not tied his ankles together and, indeed, he danced a grisly fandango."

The Reverend Cranston was as appalled by the ferocity of the crowd as by the sufferings of the condemned man. "They, who had broken bread with him, who had sipped of the evil cup with him, who had been his friends and admirers, they all now vied with each other in howling with laughter at the terrible plight of his death struggles. Never have I seen the Devil in such absolute control of a group of civilized men. Yea, it is a blessing that our days on this earth are as a shadow, and that the true meaning of the life of Man lies in Eternity, after he has been judged by God."

Departing from the scene of execution, Reverend Cranston made his way to Barbacoas by train, and then to Panama City by bungo and mule. He arrived feeling feverish, listless and dejected in spirit. Rather than stroll the sea wall with other sober-minded travelers, he chose to lie all day on his cot in the crowded hotel room, staring at the ceiling, his Bible clutched to his chest. When his ship finally arrived, his companions could not prevail upon him to stir from the bed, gather his belongings and board the ship. They had to leave him in the American hospital in Panama City. In the hospital Cranston ate barely enough to stay alive and refused even to speak or look after himself. His frame became emaciated and his beard grew long and tangled. One night he disappeared from the hospital, barefooted and wrapped in a blanket, leaving all his earthly possessions behind except his Bible. It was a relief to be rid of him because his hospital bed was badly needed. A clerk from the consul's office collected Cranston's belongings and placed them in storage. Several days later travelers found what was left of his body on the Gorgona trail, a few miles from Panama City. His Bible and a crude cross fashioned from tree branches lay on the ground beside him. No one knew where he intended going when he left the hospital. Perhaps, wrapped in a ragged blanket, bearded like a patriarch and carrying his cross, he had been seeking his Redeemer in the wilderness. When the consular clerk packed Cranston's belongings to send back to relatives in Rhode Island, he noticed that the last rational notation in the clergyman's journal had been written just after viewing the execution of Timothy Copeland. The event seems to have unhinged him. The sins of mortal men, too enormous for Isaiah Cranston, had hastened him into eternity.

Not long after Copeland's execution there was a hastily called meeting of the Isthmus Guard in the back room of the Runnels Express Service in Panama City. News had just been received that seven miners returning home from California had been brutally murdered and robbed on the jungle trail between Cruces and Panama. A vote was taken and a decision reached. Runnels brought the ledger from the vault, consulted the list of names and made assignments. That night the company stables again were empty and there were hoofbeats, snorting horses and the creak of saddle leather on the trails. Another mass roundup was in progress. When the sun rose over the Panama City sea wall next morning it revealed the bodies of 41 men hanging by the neck from the timbers projecting from the wall. Among them were five named as the murderers of the seven Californians. No prominent individuals were included in this group. These were the riffraff swept up from the back alleys of the towns and the thickets of the jungle trails.

The second mass execution was applauded by the *Star & Herald* as a work of civic merit and even as a manifestation of the Monroe Doctrine. "We have said before and we say again that the sooner the Isthmus becomes completely Yankeeized, the better it will be for everyone," said the newspaper. "We rise to say that if the work of Mr. Runnels is allowed to continue, and bear its deadly fruit—if we may assay a bit of grim humor—we may soon see the dawn of a new era when the rights of God-fearing, law-abiding, *civilized* citizens will be fully protected according to the principles laid down by the late President Monroe."

The native-born Panamanians were not quite so enthusiastic. As Runnels rode by, they avoided his gaze and kept their distance. *"El Verdugo,"* they called him—"The Hangman."

In the peaceful hiatus following the mass executions the railroad company directors suddenly terminated the quarrel between President Young and Totten by kicking Totten upstairs to superintendent of the operating section of the road and hiring Minor C. Story of Poughkeepsie, New York, to build the Barbacoas bridge and complete the tracks the 21 miles to Panama City for the sum of $3,500,000. Story had achieved success in building railroads and canals in the United States at such an early age that he was widely publicized as a boy wonder. During 1850 and 1851 he was reported to have over 6,000 men working for him on various projects scattered about the United States. George Law was highly impressed with Story and put him forward as the man to snap Panama Railroad construction out of its doldrums. By the middle of 1852 Law's voice was powerful in formulating company policy. He had invested over $500,000 in stock of the company and purchased large tracts of land on the Yankee Strip. Law convinced William C. Young, the company president, that Story was the man to finish the job, and Young convinced a majority of the board of directors. Despite the fact that he had never fulfilled a contract in the tropics before, Story did not doubt his own ability. He arrived on the Isthmus like the general of a conquering army, with bands blaring and a welcoming committee of dignitaries waiting on the wharf. After unloading a cattle boat filled with Irish laborers from County Cork, he requisitioned a train for the trip to Barbacoas and began at once to push a wooden-trestle bridge across the Chagres. It was the dry season; the river was a placid, lazy trickle in the deep channel.

Although they applauded Story's energetic attack on the bridge problem, the permanent Yankee residents of the Strip, inpatient for the railroad to be completed, were not impressed by his progress on the remainder of the road. The *Star & Herald*

Yankee Chagres during its heyday in 1850.

ABOVE: *Argonauts on the Battery at Panama City awaiting the arrival of California-bound ships.* BELOW: *Panama City in the 1850's.*

Attack on Yankee passengers in the Panama railroad station during the Watermelon War, April 15, 1856.

Train wreck at Gatun Bridge, 1853

of March 11, 1853, described the antics of Story's people mapping the route between Barbacoas and Panama City: "Engineers who perform mysterious evolutions . . . looking through complicated instruments at long staffs, driving stakes into the ground, rushing about woods and swamps in all directions . . . and then disappearing as secretly as they arrived." The newspaper lamented that there were "no stalwart laborers at work making the forest ring with the stroke of the axe." Despite all the grand talk and bustling activity, the right of way from Barbacoas to Panama City, the newspaper said woefully, "remained the birthplace of tropical vegetation and the haunt of the beast of prey."

When George Totten saw for the first time the bridge that Story was building, he was almost overcome with dismay. "It is even more fragile than I could have imagined," he wrote the company directors in New York. "It cannot possibly survive a ten-foot rise. It is an invitation to disaster."

Totten's warning went unheeded. If the directors read the letter, they ignored it. They were too busy, buying up shares and dreaming of the big boom that would come when the first train crossed the Chagres and made the dash over the Continental Divide and downhill to the Pacific Ocean.

Minor Story, directing operations in a huge cork helmet with his face hidden behind a veil of mosquito netting, had his bridge almost completed when the first rains began. High in the mountains to the south massive clouds began gathering about the peaks, black clouds filled with the mutter of thunder and bright flashes of lightning. The river water took on a sudden life, splashing over the rocks of the stream bed and casting up high waves on the sides of the deep channel. The water level had risen barely five feet when the workers on the bridge spans began noticing a heavy vibration. The construction foreman walked across slowly, and then returned to confer with Story. He expressed anxiety. Story confidently overrode the foreman's fears. "We must expect a certain amount of vibration, even sway," he said. There came an ominous cracking and crackling from the bridge. As Story and the foreman gazed, a span slowly and ponderously gave way and dropped into the river, to be swept away on the crest of the rising flood. There was a terrified scramble shoreward by the workers. They all made it, just in time. Then, with agonizing slowness, the structure began disintegrating, a span at a time, until the entire bridge, except for the shore-based pilings at each end, had disappeared.

The bridge collapse was the climactic disaster of several which occurred during the period of the Story contract. His labor force, mostly Irish, were unused to the tropical climate. Poorly housed and looked after, they suffered many casualties to fever and heat stroke. At the time the bridge collapsed, Story was down to a skeleton crew of workers. By the end of the year not a tenth of his contract had been finished, so the railroad company had to give up on him. The *Star & Herald* rejoiced with the lead: "Story is pushed overboard! Hurrah! Hurrah!" President William C. Young, who had personally sponsored Story and his wooden bridge, was forced to resign. David Hoadley succeeded Young as president of the company.

The Chagres destroyed not only Story's bridge, but his career as well. He departed from Aspinwall quietly; no band played nor committee waved goodby. He was bankrupt financially, tarnished in reputation and broken in spirit. Story spent the rest of his life trying to live down his Panama failure. And it was indeed a failure. After almost a year's work railroad construction still stood at the same point that he had found it. The Chagres was unspanned at Barbacoas and the right of way to Panama City was still a wilderness—"the birthplace of tropical vegetation and the haunt of the beast of prey."

One of the first acts by David Hoadley as President of the Panama Railroad Company was to request George Totten to resume the position of chief engineer in charge of construction. Totten did not leap at the chance. "As you well know, or probably have been informed," Totten wrote Hoadley, "I have strong views regarding the type of bridge that should be built at Barbacoas."

Hoadley answered quickly, "I have an opinion, expressed

unanimously by the board of directors, which holds that George M. Totten, chief engineer in charge of construction, will design and construct the type of bridge at Barbacoas that he believes will successfully withstand the ravages and onslaughts of the river. The board has expressed, unanimously, the utmost confidence in the ability of the said Mr. Totten to build this bridge, and enters the prayer that construction begin and proceed as quickly as possible."

Totten's return as construction chief was reported by the *Star & Herald* as having "a magical effect" on Yankee Strip affairs. The newspaper, reporting that "merchants' purse strings have been loosened" in the wave of optimism, predicted completion of the railroad within ten months and a glorious future for the Isthmus. "Where will the Nicaragua Transit be then?" crowed the newspaper.

Totten set up an iron hut at Barbacoas for a headquarters and took charge of construction again. He sent agents on the company ships all over the world to recruit laborers. Iron was heavy and needed many hands. Irish, English, French and Germans and other Europeans answered the call. From the Orient came Hindustanis and Malaysians. Pushed by a 1,000-man labor force, Totten's bridge slowly and ponderously began crossing the Chagres.

While Totten struggled with the Barbacoas bridge, disasters did not cease. On October 1, 1853, a train—locomotive, tender, four baggage cars and two crowded passenger cars—left Aspinwall at 3:30 p.m. for the scheduled run to Bohío. As the locomotive rounded the curve to cross the bridge at Tabernilla, the engineer tooted his whistle shrilly and set his brakes. A bull stood on the track in the middle of the bridge, snorting and pawing, refusing to retreat. With whistle sounding and iron wheels screeching on iron rails, the locomotive crashed into the ravine. Cars were smashed and the locomotive boiler burst in a great shower of steam. Only two passengers were killed, but several others suffered fractured bones and burns from the scalding steam.

Despite the disasters, persistence was paying off and progress was being made. In the *Star & Herald* of October 29, 1853, Totten reported that the seven miles of grading from the Chagres to the Obispo River was nearly finished and already three miles of track had been laid. The construction chief said he expected the Barbacoas bridge to be finished by December 1, which would permit trains to run past Gorgona to the Obispo River by January 1, 1854. When the tracks reached the Obispo, he planned to transfer passengers and freight directly from the steam train to a pack train. He estimated the Isthmus crossing then would take only 12 hours. The reporter obviously had found the chief engineer in a talkative mood. Totten said that grading and clearing of the right of way along the Obispo and at Panama City had already begun and that of the total 48 miles of railroad as projected, 23 miles were in operation and 30 miles would be in operation by January 1, leaving 18 miles to go. He would cut a notch, said Totten, 24 feet deep and about 1,300 feet long, in the Continental Divide at Summit. The total excavation for this notch would be 30,000 cubic yards, and it would lower the maximum elevation of the road to a level just 250 feet above Pacific high tide.

Totten estimated that if he could obtain 4,500 more men for labor, he could complete the railroad within six months—by August 1854. He said it would cost from $15 to $50 each to import these workers, a cost additional to wages and medical care expense. In speaking of medical care, Totten paid lip service to the propaganda which played down the seriousness of health problems on the Isthmus. He said reports of sickness were exaggerated and there was no reason for workers to fear that they would die of disease. Totten did not mention the funeral trains which ran daily to the cemetery at Mount Hope and the constantly expanding field of white crosses in that burial ground.

Totten said expansively that the operating section of his road, employing 1,400 men, was "as perfect a road as can be found in the United States." The railroad had eight locomotives, twelve passenger cars, 100 flatcars (called platform cars in that day), 100 dirt cars (gondolas), a foundry, carpenter shop and blacksmith shop.

While this interview was being conducted on the platform of the railroad station at Aspinwall, the news reporter found "the snorting of the iron horses very disturbing."

During October of 1853, when Totten gave this interview, crossing the Isthmus by train, boat and mule required 36 hours. Most of this time was consumed riding muleback over the muddy, vexatious Cruces road. In an attempt to reduce travel time over that section of the transit, Totten sent a group of laborers to widen and repair the road and convert it into a decent highway.

Construction work on the Cruces road bred some of the first labor unrest on the Isthmus. Totten paid the road laborers a regular wage of 80 cents a day, and promised a bonus of 40 cents a day extra to every laborer who would sign up to work on railroad construction after the highway work was finished. The alcalde at Cruces, whose name does not survive in any known record, decided to exploit the situation for personal gain. He told the work crew that if 150 of them would give him a dollar apiece, he would use his official authority to force the railroad company to pay them $1.20 a day starting at once, regardless of whether they chose to stay on with railroad after the highway work was finished. The workers agreed, took up a collection, and presented the $150. A few days later, when Totten appeared in Cruces to inspect the repair project, he was arrested by local soldiers on order of the alcalde, manacled and hustled through the streets to the jail. The alcalde sent word to railroad headquarters on Manzanillo that Totten would be released when the pay raise was forthcoming.

Shortly before noon on the second day of Totten's confinement, the hoofbeats of a dozen heavily armed riders clattered across the plaza in Cruces. The sweating horses had obviously been ridden hard. Randolph Runnels had heard of the affair in Panama early that morning and had come at once. He reined in his mount at the construction foreman's shack and looked over the idle group of workers. Runnels said quietly, "You men have sixty seconds to get back to work." There was a sudden, energetic movement for picks and shovels. Arming himself with a 20-pound sledgehammer, Runnels headed for the jail. A jingle of spurs sounded as he strode across the damp stone floor to the barred door, and then came a violent crash of steel against iron as he smashed the lock with the sledgehammer. While this was going on, the barefoot soldiers stood in the street under the drawn guns of the riders.

On Runnels' command two of the riders went to the alcalde's home, found him cowering under a bed and dragged him, kicking and struggling, through the dusty street to the whipping post in the plaza. There he was triced up by the wrists and his shirt torn off. Runnels gave him twenty lashes with a drover's whip, the blows sounding out solidly, followed by grunting screams of pain.

After the beating, Runnels left the official hanging on the post and wrote a message in both Spanish and English on a piece of paper which he nailed up in a public place. "This man was punished for interference in the peaceful and legal business of road building. Next time, he and anyone who helps him will get killed." The notice was signed with a flourish, "R. Runnels." Then with Totten bobbing uncomfortably in the saddle of one of the horses, the group rode out of town. That ended the labor dispute at Cruces, but work on the road had been delayed two days.

Totten completed the Barbacoas bridge during the last week of November 1853, beating his deadline of December 1 by several days. The bridge was of boiler iron, 625 feet long, 18 feet wide, standing 47 feet above the normal stage of the river. The ends rested on abutments of hewn masonry, 26 feet wide and 8 feet thick. Between the two abutments stretched six iron spans each more than 100 feet long. The spans rested on five masonry piers, 26 feet long by eight feet wide, firmly implanted on the river bottom. Each span had two top and bottom cords—the top cords arching upward slightly—of iron two feet wide and one inch thick. These cords were joined together with an iron web nine feet high at the center of the span and seven feet high at the ends. The tracks rode on iron floor girders, three feet apart.

The first locomotive—a 35-ton Norris with Totten at the throttle—crossed the bridge on November 26, 1853, when the river was 29 feet above its normal level. After crossing once and returning, Totten ordered a string of loaded gondola cars coupled to the locomotive and told the engine driver to take the throttle. As the locomotive chugged slowly across the bridge pulling the train, Totten watched tensely from the cab. There was a noisy clattering and clanging from the iron floor girders as the wheels rolled along, and a thump-thump-thump from the masonry piers as the locomotive and individual cars passed over them, but there was no tremor or sway in the spans. Far below, the surging waters of the Chagres splashed with futility against the bases of the piers. When the last car was safe on the opposite side, Totten slapped the engine driver on the back and laughed. His bridge was a permanent fixture on the Panama Railroad.

The *Star & Herald* was ecstatic in its reaction. "The Rubicon is passed! This day at 11 o'clock a.m. precisely, the pilot train passed over the great bridge at Barbacoas with flying colors. There were one locomotive and nine cars, heavily laden with freight and passengers. The Rubicon is passed! The Rubicon is passed!"

XI

The Canal Nightmare

DESPITE THE PROSPECT THAT THE RAIL LINK ACROSS PANAMA SEEMED destined for eventual completion, the search for an all-water route across from sea to sea still went on. Rumors had persisted for years that such a passage, or passages, did exist, and since the innumerable bays and inlets of Central America had been only lightly explored, no one could say with absolute certainty that one did not. In the United States and Europe promoters smitten with the canal dream studied the journals and maps of those who had explored the area since early times, fervently hoping to find a waterway, or what was more likely, a spot where a waterway could be dug through with a minimum of excavation. The coasts were riddled with possibilities. Gerstle Mack, the well-known historian, has said, "From Tehuantepec to Buenaventura, a span of more than 1,200 miles, almost every bay and inlet and river and mountain pass that appeared to offer the faintest promise of a feasible canal site became at one time or another the scene of wordy battles between its enthusiastic partisans and its equally vociferous opponents."

To the directors and stockholders of the Panama Railroad Company the canal dream was a nightmare. If a waterway were found or a canal dug, the result would be catastrophic. The vast expenditure of money and time in Panama would have been for nothing. The hundreds who slept in Mount Hope would have died in vain. No railroad could possibly compete with a waterway allowing ships to pass back and forth between the oceans. Docks, tracks, sheds, bridges and station houses in Panama would all fall apart from disuse and the jungle would return to cover them up. The glory of the Yankee Strip would become a memory.

The principal source of waterway stories was the writings of Baron Alexander von Humboldt, who had explored the coasts of Central America at the turn of the nineteenth century. Humboldt had not found a natural waterway, nor did he profess to have found one, but he described in his writings nine areas where *he had heard* that the possibility of finding or digging one existed. Among the nine were Nicaragua, Panama, and the Atrato River region of the New Granadan province of Choco near where the narrow appendage of Central America joined the continent of South America. This last area, although it had never been systematically explored, was the one which worried the railroad builders most during 1852.

Humboldt said that during his explorations he heard a persistent story about a village priest who had allegedly cut a passage between two rivers in this region. "In the interior of the province of Choco," wrote Humboldt, "the small ravine of Raspadura unites the neighboring sources of the San Juan River and the small river Quito. . . . A monk of great activity, curé of the village of Novita, employed his parishioners to dig a small canal in the ravine . . . by means of which, when the rains are abundant, canoes loaded with cacao pass from sea to sea. This internal communication has existed since 1788, unknown in Europe. The small canal of Raspadura unites, on the coasts of two oceans, two points 75 leagues distant from one another." The existence of the canal of Raspadura became a fixed certainty in the minds of many enthusiastic dreamers.

The Atrato, principal river of the Choco province, empties into the Caribbean at the Gulf of Urabá, a deep notch on the northern coast of present-day Colombia. According to the story heard by Humboldt, one could progress upstream on the Atrato to the provincial capital of Quibdó where the river divided into two branches. The eastern branch retained the name Atrato, and the western branch became the Quito. Following the course of the Quito one would find that its source was separated by only a narrow ridge from the headwaters of the San Juan River which flowed down the opposite slope of the divide to reach the Pacific Ocean at Buenaventura. It was in this narrow ridge between the headwaters of the two rivers that the monk in 1788 was supposed to have found the ravine which he and his parishioners deepened into the small canal.

Of course, there were rumors of other such passages. At any point where only a narrow ridge separated the sources of two rivers which flowed into opposite seas, a tradition of portage across the ridge was sure to arise. The Raspadura canal story was more widely accepted as fact than the others because it had been first told by Humboldt, the noted German naturalist, traveler and statesman, who was respected to the point of veneration in the nineteenth century. In 1852 Humboldt was a very old man, but still intellectually alert. Rumor had it Humboldt was convinced that the village priest had indeed made a canal link between the Atlantic and Pacific oceans through the ravine of Raspadura, and that the waterway was still in existence.

Among those anxious to locate and exploit this canal was a New York capitalist described by one of his contemporaries as "the mystical and imaginative Frederick M. Kelley." Kelley had the gift for acquiring hard cash in large sums with which to implement his mysticism and imagination. During the latter half of the nineteenth century he financed several expeditions to Central America seeking canal routes. In June of 1852 he sent John C. Trautwine, formerly employed in the construction of the Panama Railroad, to make a survey of the Atrato River valley and attempt to find the Raspadura canal or a similar waterway. Accompanied by Henry McCann, a surveyor, and Dr. Mina B. Halsted, a physician and botanist, Trautwine journeyed to the Gulf of Urabá and began the 220-mile trip upriver to the town of Quibdó. The hardships exceeded any that he had previously experienced in Panama.

Traveling in a 68-foot bungo, Trautwine reported his progress "at an average rate of between 7 and 10 miles per day; almost daily exposed alternately to the fierce rays of a tropical sun, and the thorough drenchings of tropical rains . . . literally 'cribbed, cabined, confined' in an oven, the heat of which was scarcely endurable, and reeking with that villainous compound of smells which codfish, semi-putrid jerked beef, unearthly cheese, and other odorous abominations of the cargo exhaled day and night; sleeping . . . on a piece of thin floor matting spread over the loose boards of the cabin floor, and shared in common by roaches, whose name was legion; tormented almost into sickness and fever by insects of microscopic dimensions, but of gigantic biting powers; constantly drinking warm water from the river, mixed with the frightful rum of the country (most appropriately called *mata burro* or 'kill donkey') eating our meals in a cabin three and a half feet high . . . where our eyes were generally regaled with the smoke from the cook's fire, or offended by hind-shortened views of our black cook himself, perfectly naked, sitting in the entrance to our cabin, perhaps paring his toenails or picking his teeth with one of our forks, or vigorously scratching his well-populated head over our stereotyped dessert of boiled rice."

The Atrato, sometimes over 100 feet wide, was overhung by a thick cover of tree branches and undergrowth, making the stream resemble a water-floored tunnel. The crew of polers had to be constantly alert for snakes coiled in the branches above, because when dislodged by the ends of the pushing poles, the reptiles frequently fell into the boat. "We kept our guns ready loaded . . ." wrote Trautwine, "and killed several almost every day, to the great gratification of the crew, who always evinced their pleasure by loud 'vivas.' Those we shot were generally from four to six feet long."

Wasps were another hazard. Their great bomb-like nests hung in the trees, filled with drowsy humming, ready to explode into a ferocious swarm on slight provocation. When approaching a nest, the crew, who were almost constantly singing otherwise, would become suddenly silent. As they drifted past, they were careful that their poles did not touch a single branch of the tree holding the nest. When that happened, the results were drastic. "Never before had I observed such hellish fury as that of an aroused wasp swarm," wrote Trautwine. "One can only wrap in a blanket cocoon and pray for their attention to be diverted elsewhere to another victim."

There were many other annoyances besides the wasps and snakes, especially the "insects of microscopic dimensions, but of gigantic biting powers," alluded to by Trautwine. Their first time ashore the white men noticed their hands and arms covered with what appeared to be a vermillion dust which they first thought was the pollen of a flower. "Yavís. Yavís," said the native polers obscurely. When the dust caused intense itching, Trautwine brought out his magnifying glass and saw that it was not dust at all but a myriad of tiny red ticks. The yavís caused such itching and irritation that Trautwine and his companions were unable to sleep for several nights. They rubbed their bodies with mixtures of brandy, tobacco, red pepper, oil and other ingredients, but nothing brought relief.

Trautwine's bungo pulled a small canoe astern which was used to explore the streams flowing into the Atrato, and occasionally as a towboat to pull the larger craft loose when it became stuck on submerged obstructions. "The floors of these streams must be ribbed with layer upon layer of sunken trees and rocks," said Trautwine, "making any attempt to dredge them deeper a task of great difficulty."

They arrived at Quibdó, the provincial capital, during the first week of August. The town, standing in the middle of a marsh that was almost a lake, presented a melancholy appearance. Several of the central buildings were of mortar and heavy wood, but most of the dwellings were palm-thatched huts. When they tied up, they found no wharves at the landing, "just a few stout stakes driven into the mud on which to tie the boats." The river banks, five to six feet high, were so muddy and slippery that one had to crawl up them on hands and knees or slide down on his haunches. Even during the "dry" month of August rain fell so copiously that the town area was a sea of mud, cross-hatched with drainage ditches overflowing with water. The inhabitants built their homes on poles six to eight feet high in an attempt to remain above the flood level, and on their feet when walking about wore shoes with wooden clogs that made them appear to be walking on short stilts. Trautwine found that food was in short supply, that the natives were even more lethargic than those of Panama, and that disease, especially that of the venereal type, was rampant. "The horrible manifestations of the sores on their visages and bodies was a sad commentary on their morals," said Trautwine like a true Victorian.

The engineer and his companions took a house in Quibdó and headquartered there for several weeks, making exploration trips up the various rivers and over the high, cloud-hung ridge which formed the divide between the oceans.

Shortly after his arrival the engineer conferred with Father Ochoa, a local priest reported to be learned in the history and geography of the region. The information Trautwine obtained caused him to question the value of the local clergy as reliable sources in these matters. Father Ochoa said that the highest ridge separating the headwaters of the Atrato and the headwaters of the streams flowing into the opposite ocean was only 18 feet above the river banks. Following the priest's directions, Totten and his guides began climbing, and finally reached the crest—700 feet above the Atrato. Finding there a narrow path, two to eight feet wide, which followed the crest, they spent several hours walking its course. Cliffs dropped away steeply on each side of the narrow path. Trautwine suffered hideously from vertigo, but refused to turn back or be carried. With his head swimming dizzily he crawled past the narrowest places, his face close to the ground, "fighting off an almost irresistible urge to throw myself over the edge."

Dr. Halsted, unaffected by the heights, leaned far out over the brink at several places to drop lines to measure altitudes. When he did this, Trautwine had to close his eyes and "hug the earth for dear life, or I would have most certainly lunged into space, and, in all probability, have taken Dr. Halsted down to eternity with me."

Trautwine forced himself to explore the entire dividing ridge in the area of Quibdó, crossing back and forth between the headwaters of the streams three times. He came to the conclusion that the Atrato river system certainly did not offer a practicable route for an interoceanary canal. The soil was too marshy to form canal banks; the rise and fall of the river levels would soon undermine them. Also, there was no stone or timber fit for construction available. In Trautwine's opinion the torrential rains would halt work at least 300 days of the year, and the climate was so unhealthy laborers could not survive in it to do heavy work.

He expressed this opinion of the Raspadura canal story:

"Now, it is not only possible, but even quite probable, that a Cura, interested in the boating business, may have exercised a sufficient influence over some of the gold hunting members of his flock, in the immediate vicinity of the spot, to induce them to cut down a few bushes, and hollow out a short gutter between some two similarly situated little runs on top of the ridge near the head of the Raspadura; and such a ditch may have been used as part of a canoe-slide across the intervening eminence, until filled up again by the rain-washes. That nothing more *was* done, is evident from Humboldt's remark that '*when the rains are abundant,* canoes loaded with cacao pass from sea to sea to sea.'

"Precisely the same kind of a canal could now be made by a dozen expert laborers, in a few days. But if done, it would be difficult to command the energy to keep it open. A few months' rain would fill it with gravel; the people would shrug their shoulders and pronounce it a case of 'Dios lo quiere,' (God wills it) and the peones, rejoicing in the failure of the innovation, would again strap their heavy burdens to their foreheads, and trudge along contented, according to the 'costumbre del país.'

"I was at San Pablo in 1852, or 64 years after the date given to Humboldt as that at which the Cura's canal was dug; yet persons living near the spot, both before and ever since that period, told me they had never heard of it; nor did I meet with one, out of more than 50 persons familiar with the Raspadura locality whom I interrogated on the subject, that had. This is not to be construed into proof that no ditch was dug; but merely that it was a work of such entire insignificance as to create little or no impression even in a region where internal improvements are entirely unknown.

"It is to be regretted that of the various representations that have been submitted to the public, as to feasibility of the several inter-oceanic canal routes through this region, none have emanated from practical civil engineers. The authors of most of them, apparently, shelter themselves in the shadow of the illustrious Humboldt; and disregard the evidence of their own senses, in favor of mis-statements, however gross, innocently promulgated by that truly great man. Humboldt never visited any of these proposed routes, and is, therefore, no more qualified than any other person to advance arguments respecting them."

Trautwine and his companions crossed the ridge for the last time in late September 1852 and made their way down the western slope to the Pacific port of Buenaventura. The bluntness of his report as to the hopelessness of a canal project on the Atrato disheartened, but did not discourage, his "mystical and imaginative" employer, Frederick M. Kelley. Over the next 20 years Kelley financed several more canal explorations to Central America. To the end of his life he was convinced that somewhere an easy passage between the opposite oceans could be found.

The ones made most happy by Trautwine's report on the Atrato were the stockholders and directors of the Panama Railroad Company. They were especially pleased with his statement: "That road, in my opinion, is destined to remain for a long time the sole medium of ready transport between the Atlantic and Pacific Oceans."

Canal exploration also had the ability to make fools of the "practical civil engineers"—so admired by Trautwine—as well as the impractical dreamers. Dr. F. N. Otis in his history of the Panama Railroad Company published in 1861 alludes briefly to one forgotten casualty of an early expedition to an area which had been favorably endorsed as a canal route by an eminent civil engineer. In describing the cemetery at Mount Hope, Otis writes, "The late lamented Strain (whose suffering and heroism as the leader of the ill-fated Darien Expedition are still fresh in the memory of his countrymen) lies buried here."

The "lamented Strain" was Lieutenant Isaac G. Strain, USN, the leader of a U. S. military party which searched for a canal route across Darien in 1854. His tragic story combines a fatal desire for glory with the hoax of a charlatan.

In 1850 Dr. Edward Cullen, an Irish physician residing in Bogotá, journeyed to London to present a paper before the British Royal Geographical Society, a paper that ultimately was fated to cause the expenditure of a large amount of time and money in exploration and the deaths of eleven men. The doctor made an impressive appearance on the podium. A tall man of large girth dressed in the white cotton garb of a tropical explorer, he doffed a white cork helmet with a flourish before beginning to read, revealing a shock of gray hair which spilled over the back of his collar almost to his shoulders. This was an era long before the globe had become the well-traveled, well-known place that it is today, and there was an intense public interest in the lectures and books of explorers. These literary efforts, Alan Moorehead tells us, "tended to be intensely personal and were propaganda of a kind. The author pleaded his special cause, often with a note of religious or passionate conviction . . . stirring up sympathy and indignation." Dr. Cullen's experiences fitted the description. First came sympathy and applause, and later the indignation and acrimony which made him a public villain for the rest of his days.

Dr. Cullen's paper said that in 1849 he had landed at Caledonia Bay on the Caribbean coast of Darien to explore the area. (Darien is that part of the Central American isthmus which lies about halfway between Panama and the coast of South America.) Dr. Cullen said that he proceeded inland on foot from Caledonia Bay, penetrated the divide through a gap that was not more than 150 feet above sea level, and within a few hours reached the headwaters of the Lara and Sabana Rivers down which he floated to the Pacific Coast. Cullen professed to have made this crossing several times in the days that followed, and displayed a map which he had prepared of the route. The paper caused a great stir of excitement in England and elsewhere among canal dreamers. On any map the land barrier of Darien did look encouragingly narrow—less than 40 miles from Caledonia Bay on the Atlantic side to Darien Harbor on the Pacific—and if there was a gap in the highlands with an altitude only 150 feet above sea level, then canal possibilities certainly did exist.

Three British businessmen—Charles Fox, John Henderson, and Thomas Brassey—were convinced that Dr. Cullen had made a brilliant, exploitable discovery. What they did not know was that the doctor was an unmitigated liar. His report and map were fabrications. He had never personally explored the coast of Darien at all. Later historians have decided that Cullen based his descriptions and map on the untrustworthy account of Lionel Wafer, a member of a British buccaneering expedition which crossed Darien in the seventeenth century. Wafer reported that the mountains of Darien did not form a continuous dividing ridge, but consisted of a row of isolated hills with broad valleys running transversely between them. The most charitable way to explain Dr. Cullen's story would be to say that he was "gambling" that Wafer was right. But if that were so, he had made a poor bet. The dividing ridge, situated a few miles inland from the Atlantic Coast, was indeed continuous, ranging in height from 700 to 2,500 feet. Its height and continuity were permanently hidden from a distant viewer behind a dense blanket of clouds.

After spending over a year in England, making many lectures

on his "explorations" and being lionized, Dr. Cullen accepted an advance of funds from the businessmen and hurried back to Bogotá to negotiate with the government for a canal-building concession across Darien. His backers then hired Lionel Gisborne, a reputable civil engineer, to make a preliminary survey of the region. Gisborne and his assistant H. C. Forde traveled to Cartagena, where Cullen was supposed to meet them, arriving there on May 1, 1852. Cullen had not yet appeared. By June 1 Cullen still had not turned up, but Gisborne had heard of the doctor's activities in Bogotá. Cullen had been able to wangle a 99-year contract, after promising to pay the government $120,000 within a year. He was now occupied with final details of the concession. Growing tired of waiting, Gisborne hired a schooner on June 12 and sailed up the coast to Caledonia Bay. On June 17 he and his companion started inland, seeking Cullen's gap in the ridge. Finding no gap, they soon lost their way and wandered around in the thick undergrowth for two days before being suddenly halted by a large band of ferociously painted Cuna Indians. The Cuna tribe had a long-standing animosity toward all Europeans dating back to cruel persecutions by the Spanish. The tribe occupied then, and do to this day, the Atlantic seaboard of Darien including the San Blas region and the offshore islands. Inland they controlled the area for a distance about halfway across. Armed with ancient firearms, spears and blowguns, they were deadly foes in the dripping gloom of the rain forest. They guided Gisborne and Forde back to the Caribbean coast and warned them not to return on pain of death. Gisborne was deeply impressed by the experience. Having heard that the Indians on the Pacific Coast were friendlier, he decided to retreat for the time being and explore the opposite coast of Darien. He and Forde went in their schooner to Aspinwall, crossed on the Yankee Strip to Panama City, and then sailed eastward, arriving at San Miguel on Darien Harbor on June 30. From Darien Harbor they paddled up the Sabana for several miles and then proceeded on foot, hacking their way inland through thick jungle until they crossed a hilly ridge and came to a large stream flowing east and northeast. "The direction of the rising ground satisfied us that this river must flow into the Atlantic," wrote Gisborne. He was wrong. Gisborne and Forde were still on the Pacific side of the central ridge, a high barrier which they could not see because of the dense undergrowth. Believing that they were near the Atlantic and therefore in the territory of the hostile Cunas, they hurried back to Darien Harbor and returned to Panama. Gisborne finally met Dr. Cullen in Aspinwall on July 30. Their confrontation was unpleasant; in fact, it ended in a violent quarrel. Gisborne refused to reveal to Cullen the results of his Darien explorations and sailed for England to make his report to his employers.

Despite his differences with Cullen and his failure to find the doctor's gap on the Atlantic seaboard, Gisborne was enthusiastic about Darien as a site for building a canal. It is difficult to say why. Gisborne was a competent engineer with the reputation of being conservative in his estimates, and he had spent only eight days in actual exploration of Darien. This brief stay did not warrant a glowing endorsement; nevertheless, he published a pamphlet entitled "The Isthmus of Darien," a report which minimized the height of the dividing ridge and described the hydrographic possibilities in extremely favorable terms, and estimated canal construction costs at only $60,000,000. The fallacy in Gisborne's opinion lay in the fact that he had not actually crossed the ridge barrier of Darien. He only *thought* he had. So, on the basis of this misapprehension he made his public report, and it was not until two years had passed that he learned the magnitude of his error.

The British group formed a syndicate called The Atlantic and Pacific Junction Company and issued a prospectus inviting the public to put up 75,000 pounds sterling to get the Darien canal project moving. Gisborne and Forde, hired to do the surveys, readied themselves for a return to the wilderness. The public, impressed with Gisborne's favorable report, quickly bought up the stock issue. Then, in the midst of all those rosy negotiations, shocking news arrived. Dr. Cullen, who had never returned from Bogotá, was offering to sell the secret of "his" route to the *Société d'Études*, a French company, for 60,000 francs. The doctor, apparently, was becoming wary of Gisborne's growing role as company explorer and wanted to realize what profit he could before the area was inspected closely. The French company, however, decided to make its own survey of Darien before paying a large sum to the doctor for his concession.

The British businessmen were convinced from Gisborne's account that military protection would be necessary to insure the safety of any surveying group on Darien. But their government was reluctant to land a military force; the sensitive Yankees might construe the act as a violation of the Monroe Doctrine and cause trouble. Then, because of the world-wide interest in Darien as the site for a canal, it was decided to make the explorations an international project. Great Britain, France, the United States and New Granada all agreed to participate, using Caledonia Bay as the principal base of operations. From the beginning it was a vague, disorganized and headless project. In sheer numbers Great Britain was the largest participant, sending two separate units. To the Atlantic side for the Caledonia Bay penetration, the British sent the brig *Espiegle* under Commander Hancock and the schooner *Scorpion* under Commander Parsons. For operations on the Pacific, from Darien Harbor inland, the British sent the steam sloop *Virago* under Commander J. C. Prevost. The other nations all concentrated their efforts on the Atlantic side, the French sending the schooner *Chimere* commanded by Lieutenant Jaureguiberry, and the United States the corvette *Cyane* under Commander George Hollins. New Granada agreed to send Colonel Codazzi, head of the National Topographical Commission, and two assistants—Castilla and Polanco—as well as a large force of convict laborers to carry supplies.

Lieutenant Isaac G. Strain of the *Cyane* volunteered to lead any U. S. exploration party sent ashore. Strain was in his early thirties, a slender, dedicated officer, five feet eight inches in height and weighing less than 150 pounds. Since entering the Navy as a midshipman at 16, he had seen much hazardous duty on land as well as the sea. In 1845 he led an exploration party into the interior of Brazil; four years later he led another group overland from Valparaiso to Rio de Janeiro. During 1850 he had been a member of the military commission which surveyed the boundary between the United States and Mexico. Despite his slender stature, Strain was wiry and tough, with a constitution capable of withstanding rigors and hardships which could fell larger, stronger men.

Cartagena was originally designated as the meeting place for the Atlantic participants, but at the last minute the site was changed to Jamaica. The *Cyane,* already at sea, could not be notified of the change and so went on to Cartagena, arriving there in early January 1854. The British engineer Forde, who had been sent to Cartagena on the *Scorpion* to tell the Americans of the change in plans, informed Commander Hollins that Gisborne was still in Jamaica waiting for the French to arrive, and that the *Scorpion* had to wait in Cartagena to pick up Dr. Cullen, who was overdue. Forde suggested that the *Cyane* proceed on to Caledonia Bay and wait there for the British and French parties. Forde said that the British group under Prevost from the *Virago* was supposed to have begun its inland penetration from the Pacific side during the latter part of the past month, and was probably at this very time engaged in exploring the ridge of Darien. This bit of news whetted Strain's desire to lead an American party ashore at once to share in the discoveries.

Commander Hollins agreed to Forde's proposal and took the *Cyane* on to Caledonia Bay, arriving there on January 17, 1854. The New Granadan delegates, Castilla and Polanco, and the convict labor force were already camped on the beach. Hollins immediately had the New Granadans summon the Cuna tribal leaders to a parley. The Indians, intimidated by the guns of the *Cyane* and threats of reprisal for any hostility on their part, sullenly agreed to allow the foreigners to land and pass through their territory unmolested, but refused to aid them by furnishing guides or food.

By January 20 Gisborne and his party still had not arrived from Jamaica and Strain had become unbearably impatient to get ashore. Strain was one of those men formed in the mold of Humboldt, Burton, Stanley and Livingstone, who viewed any unexplored wilderness with uncontrollable longing, who were irresistibly drawn onward and onward to see where this secret river led and what lay beyond that distant hill. He transmitted his fire to a large number of the ship's company and they all begged Hollins to allow them to penetrate inland at once without waiting for the British. "They already have a party ashore trying to hog the glory," Strain told Hollins.

The problem put Hollins in a quandary. Such an independent move by the Americans was certainly not authorized in official orders. In fact, Secretary of the Navy James Dobbin had not been enthusiastic about the Darien exploration at all. He had agreed that the *Cyane* could participate—without specifying the extent—since Darien was in "the cruising area of the Home Fleet and there would be scant additional expense involved." On the other hand, Dobbin had not forbidden an independent move, and that was enough for Strain. Hollins finally acquiesced. If the Americans moved inland at once, they might make contact with the British on the ridge, or even beat them to Cullen's famous gap. In either case, they would prevent the British from hogging the glory, as Strain feared. Hollins rationalized his decision on the grounds that the British had changed the meeting place from Cartagena to Jamaica without consulting him, and he still had no idea when they intended to arrive at Caledonia Bay.

Shortly after noon on January 20 Strain led a 27-man volunteer party ashore in boats from the *Cyane*. He lost one boatload of provisions in the surf, but that did not disturb him, because he intended to return within eight days at the most. His party included the New Granadans, Castilla and Polanco, who had heartily endorsed the independent move. Prior to his departure Strain wrote a letter to Secretary of the Navy Dobbin justifying his action, stating he felt that the reported savagery of the Indians of

Darien was exaggerated. Strain might have expressed a different opinion had he known what had befallen the British party on the Pacific side just a few weeks before.

The *Virago* party under Commander J. C. Prevost had landed at Darien Harbor on December 19, 1853, and followed the winding course of the Sabana River upstream for the next fifteen days. On January 2 Prevost divided his group, leaving four men to guard a cache of provisions on the river bank while he led the remainder inland to locate and explore the ridge. After two strenuous days of hacking through undergrowth on the ridge crest and finding no altitude lower than 800 feet, Prevost decided to return to the supply camp, rest up, and then search the ridge in the other direction for a notch or pass. Prevost's group found a shocking scene on arrival at the supply camp—"the murdered remains of three of our former comrades, all lying obliquely across the road and pierced with several gunshot wounds. . . ." They could not find the body of the fourth man, and never learned whether he had been killed or taken prisoner. Fearing that an Indian ambush was imminent, they did not tarry, but hurried downriver to the *Virago,* leaving the three corpses unburied.

On January 23, three days after Strain had led his group ashore, Gisborne appeared at Caledonia Bay on the *Espiegle,* accompanied by the French schooner *Chimere.* Forde appeared almost simultaneously on the *Scorpion* from Cartagena with Dr. Cullen. Gisborne was furious when he learned that the American group had gone ashore ahead of the rest. The French also were incensed. Commander Hollins indignantly retired to the *Cyane* and refused to cooperate in any further activities. Ignoring the Americans, the British and French put 50 men ashore and began an intensive search for Cullen's gap in the ridge.

While all this was going on, Strain was leading his party up the course of the Caledonia River, also seeking the elusive gap. On the third day two officers and three enlisted men became separated from the main group, and fearing they might become hopelessly lost, worked their way back to Caledonia Bay. Strain continued inland. On the sixth day his group found a Cuna village, but as he approached, its inhabitants set the place afire and fled into the jungle. By now his rations were alarmingly short and Strain began to fear an Indian attack might be in the offing. The burning village was an ominous sign.

On the seventh day they met five Indians living in a hut in the forest who made friendly gestures and offered to guide them to a river which flowed into the Pacific. Then, next day, other Indians appeared like painted ghosts, sullen in manner and obviously hostile. The new arrivals induced the five guides to go with them, leaving Strain and his men to find their way alone. Before departing, one of the guides pointed to a nearby stream and told Strain through one of the New Granadans that if they followed it upstream to its source, they would be just below a ridge beyond which all streams led downhill to the Pacific. Fearing treachery, Strain did not follow the directions. It was a serious mistake. Had he taken the Indian's word, his group would have arrived on the Pacific Coast within a few days.

Again attempting to follow Dr. Cullen's map, Strain and his men became lost and wandered for days in the wilderness, becoming gradually weaker from lack of food. They shot a wild pig occasionally or an iguana, but most of their fare consisted of buzzards, snakes and toads. The vegetation offered little in the way of sustenance. They tried to eat the cocoanuts, but found the meat so acid that it took the enamel off their teeth.

It was an unhappy, frustrated group at Caledonia Bay. Dr. Cullen was in deep disgrace. Extensive exploration had failed to verify any of the points on his map. The two officers and three enlisted men lost from Strain's group came in to report that they had found no break in the ridge whatsoever and they blamed Cullen's map for their having become lost. Commander Hollins, still smarting from Gisborne's invective over Strain's precipitate departure, informed the British in writing that he intended to report to his government that Gisborne and "his Irish conspirator, the purported Dr. Cullen," should be held responsible if any harm came to the American party still ashore. Hollins was becoming concerned over Strain's extended absence, and perhaps beginning to fear he might be held responsible by his superiors for having allowed his subordinate to mount an independent move ashore, if anything went seriously wrong.

Gisborne, humiliated by his inadvertent furtherance of Dr. Cullen's hoax, swallowed his pride and wrote to his employers, "It is proved beyond all doubt that Dr. Cullen never was in the interior, and that his statements are a plausible network of fabrications."

Aboard the *Espiegle* Commander Hancock confined Dr. Cullen to his quarters, making him a virtual prisoner. In the middle of the night Dr. Cullen escaped to the *Scorpion* and penned an insulting letter to Hancock. The doctor was brought back to the *Espiegle*, forced to apologize to the Navy officer, and again confined to his quarters.

It must be said for the British engineer Gisborne that he was the only one to make a practical attempt to rise above the bruised feelings and recriminations of the group at Caledonia Bay and try to find Strain and his party. With three companions he set out to make the Darien crossing. Following his own reasoning and instincts, he kept west of Strain's route and soon crossed the ridge, "well over 700 feet high," and found the bodies of Prevost's men. "Their clothes and provisions were untouched, their bones still forming connected skeletons, clean picked by vultures, presented . . . a hideous appearance." He gave the bodies a Christian burial and continued on. After a five-day march he reached the Sabana River and made his way downstream to Darien Harbor, where he found the *Virago*. Gisborne had found no trace of Strain or his men in the interior.

On March 9, 1854, four skeletal figures staggered out of the jungle into the Pacific coastal village of Yavisa. They were Lieutenant Strain and three companions. Strain had left 18 men, weak with hunger, in the forest, and had gone on ahead in attempt to find food and help. Forty-nine days had passed since he had gone ashore for his eight-day jaunt in the wilds of Darien to keep the British from monopolizing the glory. After obtaining food and medical supplies, Strain turned grimly back to the wilderness to rescue his men. He finally found them on March 23 and led them out to Yavisa, arriving there on March 27.

Dr. Ross, the surgeon on the *Virago,* reported, "A more wretched set of human beings was never beheld; so emaciated were they, that, clothed in their rags, they appeared like spectres; some had retained their arms and blankets, while others . . . had thrown them away. They were literally living skeletons, covered with foul ulcers . . ."

Seven of the Strain party had died, including the two New Granadan delegates. Despite the hardships, Strain had enforced strict military discipline throughout their wanderings. Daily inspections had been held and separate campfires for the officers and enlisted men were maintained each night. Only once had this military discipline nearly failed; one man, temporarily insane with hunger, had attempted to dig up one of the corpses for a cannibal meal. He was stopped by Midshipman Truxton, Strain's second-in-command, who was forced to draw his pistol and threaten to shoot the man.

Strain and his survivors arrived at Aspinwall on April 5 and were taken to the railroad hospital, where they immediately became a center of great interest. Strain had never met either Gisborne or Dr. Cullen, but he blamed both of them, especially Gisborne, for the hardships suffered by his party. There is a self-serving and rather dishonorable ring to these denunciations. One might say that Strain's own impetuosity and desire for glory had been immediately to blame for the misfortunes of his party. If he had curbed his impatience, waited until the combined group appeared at Caledonia Bay, and then participated in the exploration in a conservative, rational manner, it is doubtful that he would have lost a single man.

But the Yankees in Aspinwall, not aware of all the facts, took up Strain's cause. Feeling ran high. When Dr. Cullen arrived a few days later aboard the *Cyane,* there was talk of lynching him. The doctor wisely stayed aboard the Navy vessel until he could find space on a steamer and flee to New York. Cullen later served as a military surgeon with the British army in the Crimean War, but this period of his life is obscure. He never lost interest in promoting canal schemes. In his old age he resided in Bogotá and Washington, and frequently bombarded various bureaus with maps, plans and diagrams of projected canals across Darien. But no one paid any attention to him. The stigma of his role in the loss of the Strain expedition made him *persona non grata* for life where Central American canal projects were involved.

Lionel Gisborne returned to England and submitted a second, comprehensive report on Darien topography to the Atlantic and Pacific Junction Company, taking full responsibility for the misleading initial one. He stated that in his opinion the height of the ridge and its width made the construction of a canal there an impossibility.

The Darien hardships shattered Lieutenant Strain's health. He had gone ashore from the *Cyane* in January 1854 a vigorous 33, and emerged on the other side of Darien two months later as an old man. His hair had whitened, his shoulders sagged, and his steps faltered. His weight diminished from 145 pounds to 75. Eating the acid cocoanut meat caused most of his teeth to fall out. "My very bowels are corroded from that hideous fare," he wrote Commander Hollins. His health improved enough during his stay in the railroad hospital for him to return to the States for further medical treatment. In 1856, still ailing, he requested return to sea duty and was assigned to the USS *Arctic* in the Caribbean. While visiting in Aspinwall, he was stricken with a mild attack of fever and died suddenly on May 14, 1857. He was buried in a section of the cemetery at Mount Hope which is reserved for members of the U. S. armed forces, a victim of his burning desire to find glory in the search for an interoceanic waterway.

XII

Beyond the Rubicon

WITH THE CHAGRES FIRMLY BRIDGED AT BARBACOAS, THE MANAGEment of the Panama Railroad Company began a last mighty drive to complete the road. Beyond Barbacoas the right of way crossed relatively easy terrain for a few miles: a broad alluvial plain to Gorgona. But on the other side of Gorgona a range of broken hills barred the way as far as Matachín. Digging through this range proved even more difficult than Totten had expected, the soil composition being igneous rock and tough clay. There was an unexpected blessing, however, in the discovery of a layer of volcanic stone of sufficient depth to justify quarrying. Totten delayed forward progress long enough to build a spur to the quarry; then he began sending back loads of rock to bolster the "soft" sections of the road.

The railroad management fretted over all delays in forward progress, including building the spur. Complete the road and then build the spurs, they ordered Totten. To their way of thinking, early completion was merely a matter of persistent work and flooding the project with laborers. The arrival of 360 more Irish in

January 1854 was the beginning of that flood. By the end of February over 3,000 workers were busy on the 18-mile stretch between the Obispo River and Panama City. The dire warnings of the perils to be faced in Panama from climate and malignant disease issued by Vanderbilt and his colleagues dissuaded many Americans from coming, but other nationalities—Irish, Hindus, Chinese, English, French, Germans, Malays—responded to the call. Workers died in large numbers, but the railroad company did its best to discredit the notion that this death rate was in any way out of the ordinary. The company's attitude inspired such statements in the *Star & Herald* as follows:

"As to all the nonsense about malaria, fever, pestilential swamps and the thousand other ills that are charged to the Isthmus, we report again, they exist no more than in any other tropical climate, and that prudence and ordinary precaution is all that is required on the part of unacclimated newcomers to our sunny shores."

In their secret deliberations the board of directors of the company must have commented upon the exorbitant toll of human life taken by cholera, dysentery, sunstroke and accidents, although such factors did not greatly worry nineteenth-century men of business, who regularly sent young children into dank coal mines and worked women in unheated, dimly lit textile mills for a few cents a day. Disease and industrial accidents were logically foreseeable. It was the unforeseen, appearing with maddening frequency, which confounded their logic and jerked at their sensitive purse strings. The tragedy of the 1,000-man Chinese contingent was one of the most dramatic of all the unforeseen disasters.

Early on the morning of March 30, 1854, the sober, right-thinking Argonauts who chose to stroll on the sea wall at Panama City rather than spend their time in saloons and card rooms were rewarded for their virtue by the sight of the clipper *Sea Witch* entering the harbor. The *Witch,* owned by Howland and Aspinwall, was 192 feet long with towering masts and a black dragon as figurehead. Launched in 1846 for the China trade, by 1854 she was a famous ship. The *Sea Witch* was the first vessel to sail from New York to San Francisco around Cape Horn in less than 100 days. Twice she had broken the speed record from Canton to the United States, and neither of these passages has ever been equalled by a sailing ship.

Many of the sea wall strollers, eager to relieve their boredom, rowed out for a closer look at the beautiful vessel and thereby suffered disillusionment. The *Witch* was filthy and stank like a slaver. She had made the run from Canton to Panama with her holds packed with Chinese coolies. Soon she was joined in the harbor by two other sailing ships, equally filthy and odorous, also loaded with the Orientals.

The railroad company had purchased the services of the coolies from a Canton labor contractor under a system similar to that of the British indentured servants sent to Virginia and Georgia during the seventeenth century. The company agreed to pay the contractor $25 a month for each man sent, and then the contractor made his own arrangements with the individual coolie —generally doling out four to eight dollars a month in wages and retaining the remainder as payment for ocean passage and food. It was a slave system, but the Panama Railroad Company was not averse to using slaves if they would help complete the road.

The onlookers on the sea wall noticed with amazement the great number of Chinese discharged from each vessel. "They must have been stowed in every available nook and cranny," reported Dr. H. D. Van Lewen after observing the debarkation. When all were ashore, they formed into a long line; and followed by a crowd of curious onlookers, they marched through the city and out the gates on the inland side. Indeed, they presented an odd spectacle. Small in stature, averaging five feet in height and 120 pounds in weight per man, they resembled a weird procession of carnival midgets in their blue pajama-like suits and large conical hats. Even their silence was impressive. The coolies marched without a word, heads bowed, their delicate hands hidden in their billowing sleeves. When they appeared at the construction site near Matachín, the Irish crews stared in ill-humored surprise and then burst out in angry cursing. Long classified as stable and outhouse cleaners in Great Britain and the U. S., the Irish had risen to the heady rank of white Anglo-Saxons on arrival in Panama and wanted everyone to know it. No other nationality displayed so much animosity toward people of darker skin and foreign ways as the Irish. Their attitude became so hostile that Totten moved the Chinese camp as far from them as possible. The coolies' nearest neighbors were a small contingent of Malays, also despised by the Irish, but greatly feared. The Malays, armed with muzzle-loading rifles and razor-sharp bolo knives, were murderous adversaries. The Chinese and Malays eyed each other warily, but maintained peace.

The quality of the Chinese work heartened the construction bosses, but infuriated the sensitive Irish even further. Their shovels took smaller bites of earth and their barrowmen took lighter loads of fill than the white crews, but they worked more steadily, without breaks to smoke or gossip. They wove round high baskets which they loaded with fill and carried balanced on their heads, to the amazement of the white overseers. These baskets they ornamented with grotesque painted symbols designed to repel the Evil Eye. Whenever one of the diminutive Chinese with a huge basket on his head trotted past an Irishman, the Irishman generally crossed himself superstitiously at the sight of the heathen drawings and swore under his breath.

Two or three times a day a Chinese cook appeared, carrying across his shoulders a long pole which held a steaming keg of hot tea slung from each end. Each coolie paused briefly to drink a small cupful, then returned to his task. As a rule, the amount of their completed work at the end of the day exceeded that of a comparable group of white workers.

The Irish also found much to criticize in the off-duty activities of the Orientals. After work they marched back to their camp where barrels of hot water awaited them. Stripping off their clothes, they soaped, scrubbed, rinsed and dried themselves with towels. They anointed themselves with scented water, and then donned clean clothes for their evening meal. After eating, they sat beside their campfires, humming songs, twanging weird melodies on stringed instruments, or twittering with bird-like conversation over interminable games of fan tan. The Irish looked upon such bathing and scenting as unnatural and "foreign."

Under the terms of the labor contract the Chinese contractor agreed to furnish cooks and mess facilities for the coolies, and the railroad company was supposed to maintain in its commissary such Chinese food as "dried oysters, cuttlefish, bamboo sprouts, sweet rice crackers, salted cabbage, vermicelli, tea, and hill rice." The contract also specified that the Chinese would have joss houses and opium. The railroad recruiters had agreed to stock the drug in the company commissary along with the Chinese food. The coolies had brought with them priests to staff the joss house who set up racks of pipes and the necessary *yen she gow* scraper tools. On Saturday nights and all day Sunday, after an 80-hour work week, the entire Chinese crew lolled about, smiling drunkenly in the sickly sweet smoke from the pipes.

The Irish, although they engaged in violent alcoholic binges during their own off-hours, were shocked by the "heathenish, idolatrous practice of opium smoking." One of their number, distinguished among his fellows by his ability to read and write, wrote a letter to a Catholic priest in New York accusing the Panama Railroad Company of trafficking in drugs. The letter appeared in the New York *Herald*. The railroad company directors were not especially concerned about the letter until a bookkeeper pointed out that the cost of the opium furnished to the Chinese amounted to 15 cents a day per man. This was an expense of $150 a day, and a criminal act to boot! They wrote Totten that the Panama Railroad Company was chartered under the laws of the State of New York, and the laws of that state forbade the unlicensed dispensing of drugs. Because of the illegality, the directors said, no more opium for coolies would be imported. Of course the laws of New York also forbade the employment of slave labor, but the directors were not concerned with that technicality.

Busy as always with many problems, Totten decided to ignore the company order, and made a note to inform the commissary that the drug was to be imported as usual. Then, before the commissary was informed, Totten was stricken with another attack of fever and no one knew of his decision.

One day several weeks later, as Totten lay on a cot in his iron hut near Matachín recovering from the fever, he was roused by someone shouting outside. "I staggered across the room on malaria-quaking legs and unbolted the door to admit Mr. Baldwin," wrote Totten. "I recall that he was pale, sweating profusely and had a look of horror on his face. 'Colonel Totten, you must come at once,' he said. 'The coolies are hanging themselves in the trees and falling on their machetes. Some are paying the Malays to shoot them and chop off their heads!' "

Totten dressed as quickly as he could and put on his sun helmet. Then, with Baldwin giving him a supporting arm, the chief engineer staggered to his handcar. As they skimmed along the jungle track, propelled by two naked natives turning a double crank, Baldwin related what had happened. The opium supply had run out two weeks before and when he tried to draw more at Manzanillo, he had been told the supply was exhausted and orders had been received forbidding the commissary to order the drug. After being deprived of opium, acute melancholia had struck the Chinese. Their work gradually slowed to a halt and this morning the mass suicides had begun.

"Should I live to be as old as Methuselah, I shall never forget the sight that met my eyes that morning," Totten wrote. "More than a hundred of the coolies hung from the trees, their loose pantaloons flapping in the hot wind. Some had hung themselves with bits of rope and tough vines. Most, however, used their own hair, looping the long queue around the neck and tying the end to a tree limb."

Crumpled Chinese bodies were scattered about everywhere on the ground like broken dolls. Some had thrown themselves violently on their machetes. Others, in the words of Totten, had "cut ugly crutch-shaped sticks, sharpened the ends to a point, and thrust their necks upon them." Still others, obviously, had been aided in their self-destruction, their heads being almost blown off or severed from their bodies. From the surrounding brush came the occasional sound of a high-pitched Malaysian giggle followed quickly by the explosion of a blunderbuss or the sickening *chunk* of a blade chopping a neck, as the Malays busied themselves earning fees.

Sean Donlan, the construction foreman, a hardened veteran of two years on the Isthmus, made a report to Totten. According to his latest count there were 125 of the coolies hanging in the trees and over three hundred more dead on the ground. Others had tied stones to their clothing and jumped into the river. Still others now were sitting in the shallow water, waiting for a freshet to come along and drown them. Donlan said he was positive that if they did not get opium, the remainder would kill themselves.

Totten staggered back to his handcar. He wrote later, "Some anonymous, grubby, ink-stained bookkeeper in New York who did not know a spiking maul from a fielding pin, who had a head full of trash instead of brains had decided to institute certain economies which had fatal results." Totten's investigation showed that the coolies' depression over the deaths of a number of their group from fever had been deepened by withdrawal from the drug to the extent that they chose suicide as the only escape from the hell of their existence on the Isthmus. Rather than be responsible for the deaths of the rest of the coolies, Totten "ordered the captain of the *Gorgona* to get up steam and pick up those sitting in the water and take them forcibly to Jamaica and there to turn them over to the Chinese colony on that island, where I hoped and prayed they could obtain their drug." This ended the widespread use of Chinese workers on the railroad construction. However, Chinese influence is obvious in Panama. Today in Colón and Panama City many houses offer glimpses of the Far East: balconies decked with screens showing gaudy dragons, and gay paper lanterns swinging in the breeze. Most of the pure-bred Chinese to be seen are men, but many of the

Negro women swing on their hips babies who have eyes slanted in the Oriental cast.

The Chinese disaster became the source of several legends which joined others in the mythology of the Yankee Strip. One story has it that since "mata" is Spanish for "kill" and "chino" means "Chinese," then Matachín was named as a contraction for "Dead Chinaman," in commemoration of the Chinese suicides. This is not so. Matachín also means "butcher" and was so named on maps drawn as early as 1678, long before the Panama Railroad or any other was dreamed of, much less constructed. Also, there is an elaborate article by one L. Simonix published in 1884 in the *Bulletin,* a publication of the French canal company, which adds to the Chinese legends with this passage:

"It is said that upon the railway of the Isthmus, which is 75 kilometers in length, there is buried a Chinaman under each crosstie." Of course this is completely untrue. There were over 140,000 crossties used in the original Panama Railroad—more if one counts those in sidetracks and spurs—and never more than a thousand Chinese employed.

The deep red-clay cut between Gorgona and Matachín, where the Chinese worked with their head-borne baskets in 1854, is still part of the railroad right of way. The area was, and still is, beautiful. Here the Chagres is joined by the Rio Obispo, its greatest tributary. The section of river is now part of the Panama Canal, and the banks are lined with the mechanical appurtenances of the waterway, but in 1854 it was a virgin wilderness. A broad lake, formed by the junction of the two rivers, could be seen sparkling through a grove of gigantic ceiba trees where monkeys chattered and swung high in the branches, and in the distance on the right of the tracks were conical-shaped hills covered with short grass and scattered palms.

Totten designated Matachín a way station and built a passenger depot there as well as a system of sidetracks to enable trains bound in opposite directions to pass each other. During the time that the tracks ended at Matachín the local residents cashed in on the passenger trade by operating stores in their huts, selling fruits, cakes and a sickeningly sweet candy called "dulces." There were also several saloons offering "English beer and French claret."

At Matachín, the passengers took the jungle trail to Cruces, where the newly improved road awaited. Even after the road was repaired, traversing it by mule took eight hours, and the baggage service was erratic and undependable. Sometimes their luggage was delayed so long that the passengers waiting in Panama missed their ships. Others sailed leaving their valuables behind. The mule drovers, knowing their days were numbered, ignored all complaints. The cost of travel from Matachín to Panama City, while the rails ended there, was $18 a person and 17 cents a pound for baggage.

Beyond Matachín the tracks turned to enter the narrow valley of the Obispo, whose course twisted so sharply that two bridges had to be built within the first mile. The right of way passed through a woodland of zapote, mango, nispero and guava. Leaving the river, the tracks climbed 60 feet a mile for the next three miles until they reached Emperador Station. The pronunciation of "Emperador" was soon twisted by the Yankee tongue into "Empire" and that is what this station is called today. Here the tracks were just short of the highest elevation of the road at the village of Culebra, sometimes called Summit. This height of elevation was approximately 40 railroad miles from Manzanillo and 12 miles from Panama City. Totten notched this ridge with a cut 20 to 40 feet deep and a third of a mile in length.

For several months in 1854, while work was being done on the Culebra Cut, this village became the railroad's Pacific terminus. Otis tells us that the town boasted of "three hotels which were imported ready-made from the States, where more than a thousand men and women often were promiscuously accommodated for the night. There were also 20 or 30 native huts, about 12 feet square, each of which was considered of ample dimension to house a dozen wayworn travelers, only too thankful to find a spot of dry ground upon which to spread their blankets." At Culebra when the tracks stopped there, according to Otis, "travelers mounted mules and floundered on through heavy sloughs, along deep ravines, over precipitous mountains, in drenching rain and scorching sun, often plundered by bandits, for the remaining twelve miles to Panama."

The travelers kept on swarming and floundering, lured by the golden promises of California. In 1853, with 23 miles of track in operation, the Panama Railroad carried 32,111 passengers. In 1854, with 31 miles in operation, it carried 30,108 passengers. By the end of 1854 the railroad company's gross receipts exceeded $1,000,000.

Leaving the peak of elevation at Culebra, the tracks began a winding descent toward the Pacific, dropping 60 feet to the mile, aiming for the valley of the Rio Grande. Just a mile below the summit the tracks skirted the base of a huge basalt cliff, the face of which was lined with great crystals, 12 feet high and over a foot in diameter, giant needles "leaning at 40 degrees from the perpendicular," according to Otis, "as they are in the Fingal's Cave at Staffa and along the Palisades of the Hudson." These huge needles of rock, volcanic in origin, no longer exist. Crushed up, they made excellent fill, and thus were quickly devoured by the insatiable swamps of the lowlands.

This area showed other evidence of ancient volcanic upheaval. James Baldwin, the methodical observer, found perfect sea shells and coral on the summits of the surrounding hills, indicating to him that the sea floor must have been raised skyward by "bubbling internal forces at some faraway time in our ancient past."

On reaching the Rio Grande, the constructors built a bridge across the deep river gorge. This was at first a suspension-type bridge, but it was later supported by high pilings. As the trains clattered across, the passengers could look out the windows and see the river, narrow and noisy, winding through the forest far below.

Following the left bank of the Rio Grande for the next four miles, the line crossed that river's principal tributaries—the Pedro Miguel, Caimitillo and Cárdenas—and then entered the beautiful valley of Paraíso. When the crews reached the edge of the broad plain of Corrisal and the swamp of Correndeu, they could see in the distance on the right the bald peak of Mount Ancón, and on the left the Cerro de Buccaneros (Hill of the Buccaneers) where Morgan and his men camped the night before they attacked the city of Panama. When the tracks passed these hills, the workers too could see in the distance the cathedral towers, red tile roofs and crumbling fortifications of that ancient city.

Living conditions in Panama City had grown progressively worse with the approach of the railroad, as the rush of gold-seekers swelled in volume. Early in June of 1853 the railroad company had increased the population with a force of laborers to lay rails from the city inland. These workers were adequately housed and fed in dormitories built especially for them near Playa Prieta. With travelers the situation was different. The hotels were practically always filled to capacity, the guests sleeping on cots ten to a room. The few restaurants, serving terrible food, were not equipped to handle all the business. Long lines of hungry travelers continually queued up outside their doors. When the city's accommodations were hopelessly jammed, as they were most of the time, the travelers set up camps in the fields outside the ancient walls. Here they lived the life of vagabonds, building huts from odd bits of lumber and canvas, and cooking over campfires, waiting for their ships to come in. Occasionally there was singing and gaiety about the fires and a feeling of comradeship, especially among the members of the organized groups, but generally their existence was miserable. During dry weather the wind blew dust clouds and swarms of insects into the camp, and during the wet season the rain boiled down in clouds, soaking the campers and making them shake with ague. With no organized disposal system, they lived in their own filth. The huge black and white vultures circled overhead constantly, looking for garbage and carrion, and bands of dogs pawed through the refuse littering the camp area; but much of the refuse stayed on the ground and rotted, with the inevitable results. Dysentery raged continually in epidemic stages. Mortality was increased by the lack of medical care. In general a stricken emigrant, traveling alone, had to shift for himself during illness. His companions, because of fear of contracting his disease or preoccupation with personal problems and ambitions, generally ignored him. J. D. Borthwick, who passed through Panama City late in 1853, had this to say:

"There was a great deal of sickness, and absolute misery, among the Americans. . . . The deaths were very numerous, but were frequently the result of the imprudence of the patient himself, or of the total indifference of his neighbors, and the consequent want of any care or attendance. The heartless selfishness was truly disgusting."

By the middle of December 1854 Totten was so certain of completing the line to the city the following month he wrote Gouverneur Kemble, a member of the railroad company board of directors, suggesting that Kemble and as many directors as possible come to the Isthmus to join in the celebration.

In this letter Totten sounds almost fatuously modest and humble. He alludes to "difficulties overcome," but says, "I am ashamed that so much has been expended in overcoming so little, and take no credit for any engineering science displayed on the work." He says obscurely that "the difficulties have been of another nature and do not show themselves on the line." The difficulties must have been those of climate and disease, but he does not say specifically.

During the early morning hours of January 27, 1855, the rail-laying gangs came in sight of each other. At midnight they met below Culebra, ten and a half miles from Panama City. As usual, a rainstorm was in progress. In the light of glaring whale oil lanterns George M. Totten swung a nine-pound spiking maul to drive in the last spike. It was four years and nine months since that May morning in 1850 when he and John Trautwine had first made their axes ring on Manzanillo to begin construction of the Panama Railroad.

Early the next morning, Sunday, January 28, 1855, a train crossed from sea to sea, the first continental crossing by a railroad train. Crowds lined the tracks at the villages to witness the event. Alexander J. Center, vice president of the company, and George M. Totten were among those riding the train, waving back at the crowds. The Aspinwall *Daily Courier* said, "the shrilling whistle came thundering over the summit and down the Pacific slope, a chariot of fire bent on a perilous journey over fearful chasms, through mountain gorges, along pleasant valleys, winding around hoary mountain tops, perched upon a narrow shelf of rock in mid-air." Not to be outdone, the *Star & Herald* marveled at the "facility with which the wild creature was handled," enthusiastically hailing the event as "the ultimate triumph of Yankee enterprise."

The date of a formal celebration was set for February 15, 1855. What this celebration was to consist of became a matter of public debate. The most popular suggestions were a parade, a dinner, or a ball. The *Star & Herald* characterized the parade as "symbolic of a funeral," and denounced the dinner idea as being "too dry." After half-heartedly approving a ball, the newspaper offered a plan it said would be much more exciting and suitable: "A trip to the Chagres and back, a breakfast, dance and lunch on the banks, all in one day—why, such a thing was never heard of before, and the mention of it would have been laughed at as ridiculous five years ago."

The celebration finally held did not conform completely to the plan suggested by the *Star & Herald*. The steamer *George Law* departed from New York on February 5, 1855, bearing 16 Panama Railroad Company representatives and guests in addition to the 457 regular passengers. As the ship left the wharf, she broke out the flags of New Granada and the United States. A crowd on the wharf waved banners and set off fireworks. The *George Law* arrived in Aspinwall on February 15 and found another crowd waiting, as well as a special train consisting of a locomotive and nine passenger cars, all decorated with flags. As the train made its triumphal passage to Panama City, there were demonstrations all along the way. Floral arches spanned the tracks at each way station and people gathered on the platforms to wave and cheer. At Gatun a large sign painted on canvas proclaimed: "The problem is solved, success ever attends an enterprising people." At Panama City a throng waited at the railroad station and a brass band played martial music between outbursts of oratory.

On the morning of the next day, Saturday, the visiting directors, stockholders, steamship agents and their guests embarked on the steam launch *Columbus* for a trip to the island of Taboga. As the crowded vessel steamed across the bay, several ships in the harbor fired cannon, and many red-shirted gold-seekers on the sea wall fired their revolvers into the air. After the visitors toured the island, Captain Wild of the British steamer *Bolivia* entertained them aboard his ship, "affording one and all a good English welcome," as reported by the *Star & Herald.* Leaving the British ship, the group inspected the new Pacific Mail steamer *John L. Stephens,* which had just made the voyage around Cape Horn to take over a scheduled run between Panama City and San Francisco. The *John L. Stephens* was considered one of the most luxurious craft afloat, having a rudimentary ventilating system and a bathroom for first-class passengers. During the launch ride to the new steamer the visitors were drenched by a heavy tropical shower, but this did not dampen their gaiety.

That evening George Totten entertained 80 guests at dinner in the Aspinwall House. The atmosphere was festive. Champagne toasts were drunk to the President of the United States, the Governor of Panama, the President of the Panama Railroad, the presidents of the various shipping companies and other dignitaries.

On Sunday the guests rested, recovering from Saturday's gala exertions. On Monday, as a concession to the *Star & Herald,* the railroad entertained with a picnic on the banks of the Chagres at Bohío Soldado. On Tuesday a special train carried them back to Aspinwall where they again boarded the *George Law* and sailed for New York.

XIII

The Last Land Pirate

THE OFFICIAL OVERALL LENGTH OF THE PANAMA RAILROAD FROM coast to coast was 47 miles, 3.02 feet. There were 26 stations on the road. The track was winding, generally taking the path of least resistance along the banks of the rivers. It crossed 176 waterways, most of which were less than ten feet wide. The train ride from Manzanillo to Panama City, when made without mishap, took about four hours.

The road was built to a "wide gauge"—five feet between the rails. The original trackage was the "U" rail, actually an upside down "U" in shape. These were held in place with thin iron "straps" fastened to wooden stringers. The rails were continually breaking loose from their fastenings, causing the released rail to snap up in what was called a "snake head." A locomotive, running into an unexpected snake head on the far side of a curve, could impale its boiler on the iron spear and even derail the entire train. While these "U" rails were in use, stopping was frequent to allow train crews to beat down the snake heads with heavy mauls and re-tie the rails to the stringers. The "U" rails were later replaced by "T" rails which had holes in their bases through which spikes could be driven to anchor them firmly to the crossties. This spiking of the rail itself eliminated the snake head problem.

All of the railroad cars, passenger and freight alike, were joined together with the primitive link-and-pin coupling device. Switchmen, then called "fielders," had to work at the ends of the cars, almost between the wheels of the moving train, to drop the coupling pins into the hooks just as the cars came together. Veteran fielders could be distinguished by their missing fingers. Fielding was the most mortally dangerous of any train crew work. They relied on the twin buffers, called drumheads, at the ends of the cars to provide a safety space when two cars came together, but if the drumheads failed to withstand the impact, the fielder was smashed to death, or knocked down between the cars to be run over by the wheels.

The road was mainly a single line of track. Four tracks were laid at Aspinwall and three at Panama City, and each terminal had a turntable for locomotives. Some of the way stations had sidings and spurs branching off the main line so that trains could pass, and several also had locomotive turntables. When the railroad began its sea-to-sea service in 1855, the rolling stock consisted of eight locomotives, 12 first-class cars, 100 flatcars and 100 "dirt cars" or gondolas. Aspinwall had a machine shop described by Dr. Otis as "one hundred and fifty feet long by fifty wide, stocked with first-class machinery, sufficient to do all the repairs required for the road." There was also a blacksmith's shop, "containing six suitable forges, and a brass foundry, with a small cupola for iron castings," and a car repair shop "one hundred feet long by eighty feet wide." Aspinwall, Panama City and the way stations all had freight houses, depots, and company houses for employees.

The Bay of Panama presented a problem from the beginning because of its shallowness and the lack of interest on the part of New Granada in dredging it out. Steamers had to lie miles offshore and land passengers by shallow-draft boats. The railroad company built a 450-foot pier, and in 1856 put into service steam launches to replace all the native lighters and bungos. The railroad company joined the Pacific Mail Steamship Company in leasing three islands in the Bay of Panama—Perico, Flamenco and Islaño. These islands offered fresh spring water, and the largest steamers could anchor safely in the lee of them during storms.

A sideline of the completion of the railroad was the stringing of the company telegraph line, linking Aspinwall, Panama City and intermediate points along the railroad. Telegraph poles suffered greatly from the insidious decay, and some mahogany poles were used until Totten introduced ones made of concrete. He stood a straight stick upright in a jointed mold 20 feet high, 15 inches in diameter at the base, and eight inches at the top. These he filled with concrete, using the stick as the central core. When the concrete had hardened, the pole looked like hewn stone and would last for years.

Although the track ran from coast to coast and a daily train schedule was maintained, construction work was by no means completed. Many of the trestles had been hastily built of the poor quality local timber and could not be expected to last more than six or eight months without replacement. These trestles spanned constantly flowing streams as well as some deep ravines—20 to 80 feet in depth—which were dry most of the year. The wooden bridges crossing the streams were gradually replaced with iron ones based on stone abutments, and many of the dry ravines were filled in with tons of rock to eliminate the need for bridges altogether. In all there were 134 culverts, drains and bridges of less than ten feet in length, and 42 bridges ranging from 12 to 625 feet in length.

Totten's estimate of the total number of the work force used during the four-year period of construction tends to be unbelievably small. He estimated this total force at 6,000 men and the deaths at 835. He broke down his mortality figures as 295 whites, 140 blacks, and 400 Chinese. These figures are obviously too low. In 1855 there were already more than 6,000 graves in

Mount Hope. Of course, others besides railroad workers were buried there, but a majority were "railroad" graves. Also, there are no figures available on the number of workers' bodies sold to medical schools. A later "official" estimate of deaths made by the railroad company set the figure at 6,000. However, several impartial authorities have calculated the deaths to have been about twice that number.

From the beginning the line was not equipped to handle all the business that awaited. The New York directors canvassed the officials on the Isthmus for opinions as to what the fares and rates should be. There is a story, perhaps apocryphal, that some railroad clerks on Manzanillo, in the middle of a champagne and quinine cure for malaria, got up an April Fool type card with outlandish rates and sent it to New York for a joke. This set forth passenger fare at $25, horses $40, mules $20, and baggage at five cents a pound. The card suggested that monthly commutation tickets be priced to permanent residents of the Isthmus at $50. Children under 12 years old were to be charged half-fare and those under six, quarter-fare. A rate of $1.80 a cubic foot was suggested for express parcels. As an afterthought, the schedule suggested that the railroad extend to pedestrians for five dollars the privilege of walking the track from sea to sea.

The directors accepted the rate sheet. Vice President Alexander J. Center said that the rates "were intended to be, to a certain extent, prohibitory, until we could get things in shape." Apparently, things never got into shape. The outlandish rates stayed in effect for twenty years. The Panama Railroad had become the newest and largest land pirate on the Isthmus.

As early as 1853 the canny Commodore Vanderbilt had decided that the completion of the Panama Railroad was inevitable and that he must worm his way into the profits. In April of that year he sold his ocean-going fleet to the Accessory Transit Company which named the line the Nicaragua Steamship Company. Several months later Vanderbilt re-entered passenger steamship competition on both the Atlantic and Pacific oceans to take on all competitors, including his old colleagues of the Nicaragua

Route. He formed the Independent Line, and since the Nicaragua Steamship Company had a monopoly on the right of way across Nicaragua, Vanderbilt began sending his ships to Aspinwall and Panama City to compete with U. S. Mail and the Pacific Mail companies. In a year's time he had given the other two lines such competition that they bought him out and paid him first $40,000 and then $56,000 a year not to re-enter the business.

The completion of the railroad virtually killed the Transit Route. Steamboat traffic on the San Juan River dwindled and the dusty highway between Virgin Bay and San Juan del Sur almost disappeared. But some traffic continued to cross there for years. Mark Twain appeared on the Pacific side in 1866, finding San Juan del Sur "to consist of a few tumble-down frame shanties—they call them hotels—nestled among green verdure and overshadowed by picturesque hills." Twain rode to Virgin Bay in a mule-drawn wagon, "a faded mud wagon—with four little sore-backed rabbits hitched to it." He found the three-and-a-half-hour wagon ride pleasant, but complained of the disfiguring effects on the countryside of the road signs put up by Yankee shopkeepers. He was quite taken with the Nicaraguan girls and commented upon their rather lax behavior. "They are virtuous according to their lights, but I guess their lights are a little dim," he said.

Twain and his party crossed the lake in twelve hours by steamer and then transferred to another, smaller steamer for the trip down the San Juan River. He reached Greytown on December 31, having spent less than 24 hours crossing from the Pacific. He complained of the hotel beds, but reported the food to be good. "We had not only the usual tea and coffee and sandwiches for breakfast, but also cheese!" Obviously, in fifteen years the service of the Transit Route had greatly improved.

The completion of the Panama Railroad caused some unpleasant economic effects on the Isthmus, especially among the poverty-ridden native-born residents. Most of those formerly employed as guides, muleteers and boatmen were thrown out of work. This encouraged internal disorder. Riots, generally directed against the Yankees, broke out on occasions. Of course, there had been anti-Yankee riots long before the railroad line was finished. The first one occurred as early as May of 1850 when the road was barely begun. A Negro boy on the street in Panama City snatched an American's wallet and fled through the crowd. After a hot chase the American and his companions caught the boy, retrieved the wallet, and gave the boy a thrashing. A mob of angry pedestrians gathered and a riot ensued. Two Americans and several Negroes were killed. This was probably the worst riot on the Strip until April 15, 1856.

On that morning nearly a thousand passengers disembarked from the U. S. Mail steamer *Illinois* at Aspinwall to make the train connection with the Pacific Mail Steamer *John L. Stephens* at Panama City. It was a clear, beautiful day and the passengers were happy to be on dry land again, even briefly. While waiting to board the train, they strolled through the Mingillo, the native market place near the rear of the freight house, where half-naked vendors sold fish, cassava, bananas, plantains and steaming bowls of the fragrant sancoche, a native stew. Everyone was in good spirits as they boarded the train, although several men in the group were unusually boisterous, having purchased bottles of whiskey and brandy. One of these was a loud-voiced American named Jack Oliver. The ride, lasting almost five hours, was pleasant. The train stopped briefly at several stations to pick up passengers, and at Matachín pulled off on a sidetrack to allow an oncoming train to pass. They arrived at the railroad station on the Panama City water front about 7 p.m. where the steam tender *Taboga,* one of the several 100-ton steam tenders recently put into service, waited to carry them out to the *John L. Stephens.* Since the tide was out, the tender was not scheduled to depart until 11 p.m., so loading the craft with passengers and freight proceeded at a leisurely pace. At 8 p.m., over 50 passengers, including women and children, were aboard the *Taboga,* while 50 yards away that many more were lined up in front of the ticket window in the railroad station waiting to have their tickets stamped.

Down the street about a block from the railroad station Jack Oliver, now riotously drunk, snatched a slice of watermelon from a Negro peddler and refused to pay the requested price of ten cents. Oliver staggered on his way with his companions, eating the melon and continuing to ignore the demands of the peddler. The peddler then drew a large knife and waved it in a threatening manner. One of Oliver's companions contemptuously tossed the peddler a dime and told him to go on about his business. Infuriated, the Negro continued cursing and threatening and waving his knife. Oliver drew a pistol and pointed it drunkenly at the peddler as his companions scattered. Another Negro grappled with Oliver, taking the pistol away from him. In the altercation the pistol was discharged, wounding a bystander in the crowd.

Other shots broke out as a large mob of Negroes charged into the hotels, kicking in doors, breaking lamps and furniture, and attacking the whites.

On observing the outbreak from the deck of the *Taboga,* Captain McLane sent an urgent message to Colonel Garrido, the chief of police, that he was afraid the mob was about to attack the railroad station. Captain McLane loaded and fused a small cannon aboard the *Taboga* and several of the passengers drew revolvers. When the squad of police arrived, they went aboard the *Taboga* at once and confiscated the cannon and the pistols of the passengers. On seeing the Americans disarmed, the native mob attacked the railroad station.

At the time there were 3,000 Americans in the town bound for California and several hundred more eastbound, having just disembarked from the steamer *Golden Gate* in Panama harbor. During the next few hours many were beaten, their hotel rooms looted, and several were killed. A large group took refuge in the railroad depot, a brick building with heavy doors which made it easier to defend than many of the other buildings. They barred the doors, barricaded the windows and prepared for attack. Joseph Stokes, the freight agent, sent an urgent telegraph message to Cruces for help. Randolph Runnels was known to be at Cruces with several members of the Isthmus Guard.

After completely disarming the Americans aboard the *Taboga,* Colonel Garrido led his constabulary force toward the railroad depot with bayonets fixed, apparently to disperse the mob besieging the building. There was a hot battle in progress. Armed members of the mob were peppering the building with rifle fire and the Americans inside were shooting back. When the mob parted to allow the soldiers to go through, gunfire from the railroad station killed one of the soldiers. At this point, according to the subsequent official U. S. report of the affair, "the police joined the people and began firing on the Depot."

Encouraged by the action of the uniformed troops, a large section of the population began an insurrection. Mobs ransacked the city for arms with which to kill the hated Yankees. Finding the military arsenal locked and barred, one group rushed to the Governor's Palace and seized Governor Aniño, threatening him with death if he did not turn over the arsenal keys. The governor, in the official U. S. report, said his words at the time of peril had been—"I know that you would murder me. I know that you have long wished for a chance to do so. But listen, all of you: before I would issue arms for any purpose except to disperse this infamous mob, I would suffer myself to be torn limb from limb."

The mob released the governor without obtaining the keys and resumed the attack on the railroad station.

The situation inside the station was becoming desperate. The howling mob beat on the brick walls with clubs and spears and fired rifles and pistols through the crevices of the barred windows. Then Stokes, the freight agent, and Robert Marks, the depot watchman, utilized the only heavy weapon they had, a rusty mortar from the old Spanish days which had been kept as a historical relic in the waiting room. They loaded this antique with black powder, bolts and rivets, and trained the muzzle on the main door of the building. Outside, the mob had appropriated a mahogany telephone pole which they were using as a battering ram, smashing the barred door with great blows. When the door seemed about to burst from its hinges, most of the Americans retreated up the staircase to the second story, and the two railroaders lit the mortar fuse.

As the station door crashed inward, there was a terrific blast, killing one of the attackers and wounding several more, but the mob poured into the building. They fought their way into the telegraph room, killing Stokes and Marks, and then dragged several men and women from hiding places under desks and in closets whom they also killed. When the mob tried to rush the stairs, they were met with such a deadly fire that they were forced to withdraw. Retreating outside the building, they cut the telegraph wires to silence the chattering key, and brought a barrel of whale oil from the dock to set fire to the stairway. But the telegraph had done its work. The incendiary endeavors on the stairs were interrupted by the sudden piercing shriek of the whistle of an approaching locomotive. It pulled a string of gondola cars loaded with armed railroad workers from Cruces, led by the white-hatted Ran Runnels. Attacked from the rear by this force, the mob took refuge inside the depot, where its members began to be harassed by gunfire from outside and the floor above. Fearing for the lives of the besieged Americans on the second floor, Runnels called out in Spanish for those who wished to surrender to lay down their weapons and come out with their hands over their heads. The rioters inside the building, recognizing the voice of *El Verdugo,* the Hangman, hastily complied, but in the confusion most of them escaped into the sympathetic throng of bystanders, and disappeared. Only a handful were taken into custody.

Amos B. Corwine, a U. S. citizen residing on the Isthmus who had experienced the horror of the rioting and observed the scene in the railroad depot shortly after fighting ceased, was appointed to make the official U. S. investigation of the affair. "In examining the railroad office afterward," he wrote, "a horrid sight presented itself, many dead and wounded, horribly mutilated lay about; the floor was covered with blood, all of the furniture, books, papers, etc. of the company were destroyed . . . the telegraph wires cut and an attempt was made to fire the Depot, but . . . it did not succeed . . . 15 lives were known to be lost, all passengers except two. . . ."

A week later Governor Aniño made an official report listing the dead as 15 Americans and two natives, and the wounded as

16 Americans and 13 natives. He denied that the police had taken sides with the rioters and maintained that the Americans inside the railroad station had been heavily armed and had fired indiscriminately at everyone outside the building, military or civilian.

Corwine's report contradicted the governor. "All of the arms in the office were a double-barreled gun, a pair of pistols, a sabre, and 14 old flintlock muskets, which were given out and loaded. An old cannon belonging to the company was dug out of the sand and loaded with rivets, but all who had authority gave positive orders it was not to be fired unless an advance was made by the mob. In the meantime most of the persons inside the station sheltered themselves as well as possible from the bullets that now flew about fast. . . . No attempt was made by the police to restrain the mob; but on the contrary, they joined the mob and began firing on the Depot." To explain why other Americans had not come to the aid of their beleaguered fellow countrymen in the railroad station, Corwine said, "Colonel Garrido had sent a force aboard the *Taboga*, disarmed the passengers and taken the ship's gun. . . ."

Corwine insisted that "the dispute relative to the slice of watermelon was seized upon as a pretext by the colored population to assault the Americans and plunder their property . . . but the assault on the railroad station was deliberately planned by the Police and mob."

Corwine's report stated that the animosity of the Panamanian population had been stirred because of widespread unemployment, caused by completion of the railroad construction work and the replacement of native rowboat service in the harbor of Panama by the *Taboga* and other steam launches, but that it did not justify the riot. The Corwine report ended with these words, "The Government of New Granada is unable to enforce order and afford adequate protection to the transit. . . . I recommend the immediate occupation of the Isthmus, from Ocean to Ocean, by the United States, unless New Granada can satisfy us as to her ability and inclination to afford proper protection and make speedy and ample atonement."

This report, issued in Washington in July of 1856, three months after the riot, caused a strong wave of public resentment against New Granada. President Polk had forcibly restated the Monroe Doctrine in 1845, and since then militant forces in the United States had used the Doctrine to justify all sorts of military adventures in Central America. Public opinion, whipped to a high pitch of excitement by heated newspaper editorials, demanded an invasion of Panama if retribution was not made immediately. Two small U. S. Navy warships, *Independence* and *St. Mary's,* were ordered to Panama City. They arrived in the harbor on September 19, 1856, six months after the Watermelon War—as the riot was called—had occurred. An armed military detachment under the command of Commander William Mervine landed and occupied the railroad station. By then the population had lapsed again into its usual sullen lethargy. All was quiet. The force occupied the station for three days and then returned to the ships. Not a shot was fired. This was the first official armed intervention on the Isthmus by the U. S. The Secretary of State justified the action under the Treaty of 1846 between the U. S. and New Granada, which said in part that the U. S. would guarantee the neutrality of the Isthmus only if "the free transit from one to the other sea is not interrupted or embarrassed."

President Franklin Pierce, after having made the token occupation of the railroad station, sent James B. Bowlin, the U. S. Minister to New Granada, and Isaac Morse to Bogotá as plenipotentiaries to demand indemnity. Heated discussions were held during February of 1857. The New Granadan government produced several foreign witnesses to the riot—other than Americans—who refuted the Corwine report by testifying that the Americans had been the aggressors, not the native population.

Ignoring the testimony of these foreigners, the U. S. plenipotentiaries made the following demands:

1. Panama City and Colón would be free cities under New Granada sovereignty and would jointly control a 20-mile-wide belt stretching from sea to sea, using the railroad right of way as the center line.

2. New Granada would cede to the U. S. the islands in Panama Bay for use of naval installations.

3. New Granada would transfer its rights in the Panama Railroad to the U. S.

4. New Granada would pay full damages for loss of life and destruction of property in the riot.

5. When the above conditions were fulfilled, the U. S. would pay New Granada $2,000,000.

New Granada rejected all the demands. The U. S. finally gave up its attempt to gain control of the railroad, but insisted on the payment of damages. Finally, in 1860, after years of recriminations and haggling, New Granada paid $412,394; but the payment was a source of continuing bitterness.

The railroad concession from New Granada prohibited anyone from building another railroad, canal or road across the Isthmus without the consent of the board of directors of the Panama Railroad Company. Thus the company had a death grip on interocean trade, just as William H. Aspinwall had foreseen. For 15 years after its completion the railroad was the most important link connecting Europe and the Eastern Seaboard of the United States with the western coasts of North, Central and South America and the Orient. Yearly the road carried more than 20,000 people each way across the Isthmus. Between 1855 and 1860 it transported over 500,000,000 dollars in California gold and more than 100,000 bags of U.S. Mail without a loss.

But for years trouble plagued the hastily constructed right of way. Bridges collapsed and landslides frequently swept away sections of track or covered them up. The roadbed was unbelievably soft in places, too soft to bear the daily burdens of the heavy trains. Only forward movement, in many sections, enabled the trains to pass safely. Ballasting with tons of rock went on continuously. The *Star & Herald* in 1858 reported an instance in which a work crew left its train standing in the Black Swamp to pursue some marmosets observed swinging in low foliage nearby. When the crew returned over an hour later with several of the tiny monkeys captured as pets, they could not find the locomotive, tender, and six gondolas. The tracks, slightly askew, were still visible. One rail, apparently, had sunk down, allowing the train to tip over, and the swamp beside the roadbed had swallowed the entire train.

Railroad ties cut from the local wood rotted with astonishing rapidity. Soaking in pitch delayed the process, but still they disintegrated in six to eight months. Totten began importing lignum vitae logs from Cartagena. This wood was difficult to work with because of its iron-like hardness, but ties made of it were almost impervious to decay. Section gangs cursed as they tried futilely to pound spikes into the lignum vitae. They had to use iron screws to anchor the rails to the ties. It was laborious to put in a tie of this wood, but once in, it was there for years. Many of these ties, dug up when the American canal company relocated the line in 1910, were found still unrotted.

The wood of the railroad cars—passenger, freight and flatcars—rotted so rapidly that a score of carpenters worked continually replacing sections with mahogany boards. Soon the carpenters had replaced all of the original wood, and the Panama Railroad Company became the only railroad in existence with solid mahogany cars.

Effective maintenance of the roadbed and equipment gradually reduced the time necessary for the interoceanic trip to slightly less than three hours. Docking and loading procedures were made more efficient, especially at Aspinwall where the railroad line ran directly to the 1,000-foot covered wharf. Two hours elapsed between the arrival of a ship and the departure of trains loaded with 400 to 800 passengers and hundreds of tons of freight. During the dry season it was not unusual for 1,500 passengers and the mail and freight from as many as three ships to be unloaded and transferred across in less than half a day.

The railroad construction account, when it was finally closed January 1, 1859, showed an expenditure of slightly more than $8,000,000, or about $168,000 a mile. The actual cost had been much more, since the $8,000,000 did not take into account the losses of Totten and Trautwine and of Minor C. Story as private contractors. However, the balance sheet issued on the closing date showed the gross earnings of the road to that time as also slightly more than $8,000,000. On paper at least the railroad had "paid for itself" within four years of operation.

The improvements and modifications on the line made between the formal completion in 1855 and the closing of construction books in 1859 were not made by issuing new stock, but by spending over $2,000,000 that the company had taken in for part-way travel prior to full completion of the line. But now that the road was paid for, it was obvious to the directors that they had found a gold mine without going to California. Operating costs amounted to slightly more than $2,000,000 for this period, leaving a difference between gross earnings and operating costs at more than $5,000,000. This profit, an enormous one in 1859, came from a railroad slightly more than 47 miles long.

The April Fool rate schedule submitted by the tipsy clerks on Manzanillo in 1855 continued in effect permanently and some charges were even raised. First-class freight shipped from New York to Valparaiso, Chile, via the Isthmus of Panama, for example—a distance of 4,630 miles—cost $30 a ton. The Panama Railroad's share of this tonnage charge was $15—half the total. Forty-seven miles by land cost as much as 4,583 miles by water. In addition to the freight and passenger revenue, the U. S. Government paid the railroad a flat $100,000 a year for carrying the mail.

In May of 1855, three months after the daily service began, the board of directors of the Panama Railroad Company met in their offices at 88 Wall Street and declared a six per cent dividend to stockholders. Three months later they declared another six per cent and three months after that, still another, making a total dividend of 24 per cent paid the first year after completion. Panama Railroad Company stock, which had sold for a few cents a share during its low point in 1852, rose to over $340 a share during the 1860's. When the construction account was closed, directors decided to compensate the stockholders for the revenues from part-way travel spent for repairs on the line. They voted a 40 per cent stock dividend to all shareholders. This announcement reach the floor of the stock exchange while Panama Railroad stock stood at $250 a share. Rumors swept the floor that the directors were "watering" the stock and speculating. The price nosedived. But the next day the market rebounded and the "watered" shares rose again to $250 each. From 1856 to 1870 the annual dividend was never less than 12 per cent and in 1868 was a phenomenal 44 per cent. During 1868 the price of the stock reached $348 a share, its highest point.

During this period of astronomical earnings there was one dark cloud on the horizon. Under the terms of the original concession with New Granada, that country had the right to buy the railroad outright in 1875 by paying $5,000,000. Since the railroad was worth easily $25,000,000, it was inevitable that New Granada would exercise the option. The directors called George M. Totten to New York for a conference and then sent him to Bogotá to negotiate a new contract on the best terms he could manage.

Bogotá, now the capital of a federation calling itself the United States of Colombia, had not learned to love the Yankees and their methods during the past decade and a half. The humiliation of the Watermelon War reparations still rankled. The government drove a stiff bargain. In return for granting the Panama Railroad Company a new 99-year lease, beginning July 7, 1867, the company had to agree to the following terms:

1. Carry Colombian mails and government employees free of charge.
2. Pay an annual subsidy of $250,000 to Colombia in addition to its three per cent royalty on each dividend.
3. Undertake millions of dollars in harbor improvements, including dredging and the construction of breakwaters, at both Panama City and Colón.
4. Pay Colombia a cash bonus of $1,000,000.

The contract of 1867 also modified the contract of 1848 by putting geographical limits on the extent of the company's area of immunity from competition from other railroads and highways. In addition, the new contract said that the right of the company to give consent to the building of a canal in Panama did not apply anywhere except on the actual railroad right of way itself.

The first provision of the revised agreement proved to be the greatest source of expense and irritation of all. Any Colombian citizen in Panama with the slightest political influence could obtain papers identifying him as a "government employee," and thereby ride the line free. Thereafter many trains regularly carried more Colombian deadheads than paying passengers. Also, Colombian politicians soon took advantage of the first provision of the new agreement to ship their farm produce and livestock free on the railroad, as first-class mail. This burden cut into the space available for revenue freight and forced the company to increase the number of daily trains.

Added to the financial burdens imposed by the revised concession were the expenses of double wages, free maintenance and medical care necessary to obtain employees. The retention of workers was a problem from beginning to end with the railroad. Despite the high wages and other benefits, the company found it difficult to keep them longer than a few weeks. California continued to beckon and every steamer leaving Panama City carried as passengers a large number of railroad workers.

The roadbed required so much maintenance that permanent gangs were assigned to each four-mile section of track to repair snake heads and replace ties. When not occupied with the roadbed, they were kept busy chopping back the ever encroaching forest and cutting wood for the fuel piles at each way station. Even considering the high wages, using local wood was cheaper than importing coal. The cost of labor, material and upkeep of each mile of track averaged more than $20,000 a year.

To transport a constant stream of worker recruits to the Isthmus, the railroad company bought ten stern-wheel steamships and established the Brig Line, operating between New York and Aspinwall. Workers signed agreements that if they worked six months on the Isthmus they would be entitled to free passage from Panama City to San Francisco on the Pacific Mail Line.

Many, too impatient to wait the six months, jumped their contracts and left for the gold fields after a few weeks working for the road. Thus the personnel turnover was extremely high, except for a few key men such as George Totten and James Baldwin, who stayed with the road for years after its completion.

The reservoirs of trade in California and the Orient were not the only ones tapped by the railroad. When the railroad was completed, California had a population of only 500,000 while Central America had 2,000,000. On the Pacific coast of South America, heretofore accessible to the Atlantic only by way of Cape Horn, were 800,000 more. Prior to the completion of the railroad 90 per cent of the trade from the Pacific coast of Central and South America went to Europe. This trade was estimated at $60,000,000 per annum.

The Pacific coast of Latin America, primitive and backward, did not at first understand the importance of the railroad, and most ports were isolated from it. Dr. F. N. Otis says, "Central American states had at that time no means of connection with the road. Their Pacific ports had been so long shut out from remunerative commercial relations that they could not at once realize the advantages the Isthmus railroad offered over the tedious and expensive land route to the Atlantic; they required to be lifted from the ruts along which they had been creeping and groaning for ages, and placed upon this great commercial highway." To help these backward countries make contact with the great "commercial highway," the Panama Railroad in 1856 organized a steamship line to service the Pacific ports from Panama north to San José de Guatemala, and a British company founded a line offering schedules south to Chile, Peru, Bolivia and Ecuador. By 1858 the cargoes from these ports had an annual value of $2,000,000. South and Central America shipped indigo, cochineal, India rubber, coffee, cocoa, hides, pearl shells, tobacco and straw hats to the United States and Europe in return for manufactured goods.

After completion of the transcontinental tracks at Promontory Point, Utah, on May 10, 1869, the importance of the Panama Railroad began waning, but it was still a profitable enterprise. Dividends paid on its stock ranged from nine per cent to 16 per cent annually.

In 1879 when the ill-fated French company was formed to build a canal across the Isthmus, the Panama Railroad Company had 70,000 shares of stock outstanding which had been selling for about $150 a share. The company offered to sell the French company a controlling amount of the stock for $200 a share. The French haughtily refused. Thereafter, the railroad sidetracked and lost many of the canal company supplies shipped in its cars. While this was going on, President Trenor Park of the railroad company and other large stockholders were quietly buying up huge blocs of shares at $150 a share. When the French company gave up in defeat and again broached the matter of purchase, they found that the price had gone up. The French finally had to pay $250 a share for 68,534 of the outstanding 70,000 shares—a total of $17,133,500—and the Wall Street men required cash, not long-term bonds. In addition, the French company had to pay off $7,000,000 in railroad company bonds and $1,102,000 for the sinking fund. This made a total price of well over $20,000,000. André Siegfried, an official of the French company, called it "a real Stock Exchange holdup."

A long-range effect of building the railroad across the Isthmus was that it gave Panama a tremendous advantage over other sites as the place to cut an interoceanic canal. Building the road educated engineers in the most minute problems of the area's terrain and climate, and De Lesseps' experience in the canal-building days of the 1880's showed that a railroad was perhaps the most indispensable of all tools necessary to dig a canal. During the early 1900's when the United States began operations in Panama it acquired the railroad, along with the other assets of the defunct French company. By then the railroad was hopelessly obsolete in both roadbed and equipment, but nevertheless indispensable. As work on the canal progressed inland from the Atlantic side, virtually the entire length of the railroad was relocated with heavier rails, standard gauge and double-trackage. Nearly half of the original right of way of the Panama Railroad lies now at the bottom of Gatun Lake. The relocated line in that area skirts the lake's eastern shore.

George M. Totten remained on the Isthmus as chief engineer of the railroad until 1875. In 1857 he had made a survey of the Isthmus for a lock canal from Limón Bay to Panama City. This survey envisioned a canal with a bottom width of 150 feet, a depth of 31 feet, and locks 400 feet long by 30 feet wide. A 24-mile feeder channel from the upper Chagres would furnish the water to raise the ships through the locks over the maximum summit of 150 feet. He estimated the cost of this lock canal at $80,000,000 as opposed to an estimated cost of $429,000,000 for a sea-level canal of the same length and breadth. Nothing was ever done to make this canal a reality, but in 1879 De Lesseps appointed Totten chief of the French company's engineers, the only American in the group.

Totten later went to Venezuela and built the first railroad from Caracas to La Guayra, another single-track nightmare, winding around mountains and spanning bottomless gullies.

For his contributions to the French canal company Napoleon III gave him a gold ring with a design of the imperial crown in diamonds. General Guzman Blanco, dictator of Venezuela, awarded him a gold medal decorated with the bust of Simón Bolívar as recognition for his work on the railroad from Caracas. The Panama Railroad never honored him in any outstanding way. There is a small plaque with his profile etched on it in the Panama Railroad station at Panama City, but that is all. Totten died May 17, 1884, in New York City. The brief obituary in the New York *Times* stated that he was a retired engineer. It failed to say that he was the man directly responsible for building the first transcontinental railroad the world had ever seen.

Bibliography

By far the most important source of information regarding the period covered by this book is *The Panama Collection* in the Panama Canal Library, Balboa Heights, Canal Zone. Scholars and other interested persons are referred to *The Subject Catalog of the Special Panama Collection of the Canal Zone Library-Museum,* published by G. K. Hall & Co., 70 Lincoln Street, Boston, Mass., 1964.

An important catalog of Congressional documents and reports is in the Library of Congress: *List of References on the Panama Canal and the Panama Canal Zone,* H. H. B. Meyer, 1919.

Available in the National Archives, Washington, D. C., are all of the business records and correspondence of the Panama Railroad Company, including communications of the board of directors to the stockholders, minutes of the meetings of the executive committee of the board of directors, reports of the chief engineer, and numerous fiscal statements.

The following is a list of the most important sources used in writing this book:

Abbott, Willis J., *Panama and the Canal.* New York: Dodd, Mead & Co., 1914.

Anderson, Robert, *An Artillery Officer in the Mexican War,* 1846-47. New York and London: 1911.

Bancroft, Hubert H., *California Inter Pocula.* San Francisco: The History Company, 1888.

Barra, E. I., *Tale of Two Oceans*. San Francisco: privately printed, 1893.

Bates, Mrs. D. B., *Incidents on Land and Water*. Boston: James French & Co., 1857.

Berthold, Victor M., *The Pioneer Steamer California*. Boston: Houghton Mifflin Co., 1932.

Borthwick, J. C., *Three Years in California*. Edinburgh: William Blackwood & Sons, 1857.

Capron, E. S., *History of California*. Boston: John P. Jewett & Co., 1854.

Castillero, R., Ernesto J., "Ran Runnels en la ruta de 'El Dorado'" (*Loteria*, 2 (no. 23) October 1957).

Caughey, John W., *Rushing for Gold*. Berkeley, Cal.: University of California Press, 1949.

Coffin, George, *A Pioneer Voyage to California*. Chicago: privately printed, 1908.

Crosby, Elisha Oscar, *Memoirs*. San Marino, Calif.: The Huntington Library, 1945.

Cushing, John M., "From New York to San Francisco via the Isthmus of Panama." (*Quarterly of the Society of California Pioneers*, Vol. VI, No. 3.) San Francisco: The Society of California Pioneers, 1929.

Cutler, Carl C., *Queens of the Western Ocean*. Annapolis: U. S. Naval Institute, 1961.

Duval, Miles P., Jr., *And the Mountains Will Move*. Stanford University Press, 1947.

Exquemelin, Alexandre Olivier, *The Buccaneers of America*. New York: E. P. Dutton & Co., 1923.

Fabens, Joseph W., *A Story of Life on the Isthmus*. New York: G. P. Putnam & Co., 1853.

Gisborne, Lionel, *The Isthmus of Darien in 1852*. London: Saunders & Stratford, 1853.

Goddard, Henry, *Memoirs of a Bow Street Runner*. New York: William Morrow & Co.

Grant, U. S., *Personal Memoirs*. New York: Charles L. Webster & Co., 1885.

Gregory, Joseph W., *Gregory's Guide for California Travellers Via the Isthmus of Panama*. New York: Nafis & Cornish, 1850.

Griswold, Chauncey D., *The Isthmus of Panama, and What I Saw There*. New York: Dewitt & Davenport, 1852.

Hale, Richard L., *The Log of a Forty-Niner*. Boston: B. J. Brimmer & Co., 1923.

Haskins, C. W., *The Argonauts of California*. New York: Fords, Howard & Hulbert, 1890.

Haskins, Frederic J., *The Panama Canal*. New York: Doubleday, Page & Co., 1913.

Headley, Joel T., "The Darien Exploring Expedition Under The Command of Lieutenant Isaac G. Strain, USN." (*Harper's New Monthly Magazine*, Vol. 10, No. 58. March 1855.)

Heald, Jean Sadler, *Picturesque Panama*. Chicago: Curt Teich & Co., 1928.

Henderson, Hulda, "Ran Runnels, Texas Ranger." (*October in Panama*, October 1950.)

Howe, Otavius T., *Argonauts of '49*. Cambridge, Mass.: Harvard University Press, 1923.

Johnson, Theodore T., *Sights in the Gold Region*. New York: Baker & Scribner, 1849.

Johnson, Willis F., *Four Centuries of the Panama Canal*. London: Cassell & Co., 1907.

Keasbey, Lindley M., *The Nicaragua Canal and the Monroe Doctrine*. New York: Putnam, 1896.

Kemble, John Haskell, *The Panama Route:* 1848-1869. Berkeley, Calif.: University of California Press, 1943.

Letts, J. M., *California Illustrated*. New York: R. T. Young, 1853.

Lewis, Lloyd, *Captain Sam Grant*. Boston: Little, Brown & Co., 1950.

Lewis, William S., "Reminiscences of Delia B. Sheffield." (*Washington Historical Quarterly*, Vol. 15 (1924) 49-62.)

Low, Garrett, *Gold Rush by Sea*. Philadelphia: University of Pennsylvania Press, 1941.

Mack, Gerstle, *The Land Divided: A History of the Panama Canal*. New York: Alfred Knopf, 1944.

Marryat, Frank, *Mountains and Molehills*. New York: Harper & Brothers, 1855.

Marsden, Octavia Charity *nee* Runnels, *Letters, Diary and Memorabilia*. Manuscript, Author's Collection.

Otis, Dr. F. N., *Illustrated History of the Panama Railroad*, New York: Harper & Brothers, 1862. (2nd Edition)

Pacific Mail Steamship Company, A Sketch of the Route to California, China and Japan, via the Isthmus of Panama. San Francisco: A. Roman & Co., 1867.

Pratt, Julius H., "To California by Panama in '49." (*Century Magazine,* Vol. XLI, No. 6.) New York, April 1891.

Ringwalt, John L., *Anecdotes of General Ulysses S. Grant.* Philadelphia: 1886.

Robinson, Tracy, *Fifty Years at Panama.* New York: Charles Scribner's Sons, 1920.

Robinson, Tracy, *Panama, A Personal Record of Forty-Six Years,* 1861-1907. Panama: The Star & Herald Co., 1907.

Ross, Ishbel, *The General's Wife.* New York: Dodd, Mead, 1959.

Stephens, John Lloyd, *Incidents of Travel in Central America, Chiapas, and Yucatan.* New York: Harper & Brothers, 1841.

Strain, Isaac G., "Letter to Commander Edward Marshall, R. N., HBM's Ship Virago." Panama: Daily Panama Star, April 18, 1854.

Taylor, Bayard, *Eldorado.* London: Richard Bentley, 1850.

Tomes, Robert, *Panama in 1855.* New York: Harper & Brothers, 1855. (Contains portrait of Ran Runnels.)

Trautwine, John C., *Rough Notes, on an Exploration for an Inter-Oceanic Canal Route by Way of the Rivers Atrato and San Juan, in New Granada, South America.* Philadelphia: Barnard and Jones, Printers, 1854.

Tripler, Dr. C. S., *Report of Regimental Surgeon, 4th Infantry, to Surgeon General, September 14, 1852.* (*Panama Canal Record,* VI, July 1, 1908.)

Tripler, Eunice, *Eunice Tripler: Some Notes of Her Personal Recollections.* New York: 1910.

Wiltsee, Ernest A., *Gold Rush Steamers,* San Francisco: The Grabhorn Press, 1938.

Periodicals Consulted

Star & Herald, Panama

Daily Courier, Colón

Panama American, Panama

Panama Canal Record, Mount Hope

Bulletin du Canal Interocéanique, Ancon

The Times, London (microfilm, University of Texas, Austin, Texas)

Index

INDEX

A

B